TEACHING AND LEARNING
TEAM SPORTS
AND GAMES

D0002462

Jean-Francis **GRÉHAIGNE**, Jean-François **RICHARD**,
AND Linda L. **GRIFFIN**

RoutledgeFalmer

NEW YORK AND LONDON

Published in 2005 by
RoutledgeFalmer
Taylor & Francis Group
270 Madison Avenue
New York, NY 10016
www.routledge-ny.com

Published in Great Britain by
RoutledgeFalmer
Taylor & Francis Group
2 Park Square
Milton Park, Abingdon
Oxon OX14 4RN
www.routledge.co.uk

10 9 8 7 6 5 4 3 2 1

Library of Congress Cataloging-in-Publication Data
    Gréhaigne, Jean-Francis.
        Teaching and learning team sports and games / Jean-Francis Gréhaigne,
    Jean-François Richard, Linda L. Griffin.
            p. cm.
        Includes bibliographical references and index.
        ISBN 0-415-94639-5 (hb : alk. paper) — ISBN 0-415-94640-9 (pb : alk. paper)
        1. Sports–Study and teaching.   2. Teamwork (Sports)—Study and teaching.
        3. Group games–Study and teaching.
    I. Richard, Jean-François, 1966–   II. Griffin, Linda L., 1954–   III. Title.

    GV361.G74 2004 2005
    796'.071—dc22   2004012244

DEDICATION

This book is dedicated to the memory of my father, Adelin Richard (1919–2003), whose simple and unselfish approach to life is the greatest education I could have ever received.

Jean-François Richard

This book is dedicated to teachers and coaches willing to embrace a constructivist approach to learning sport-related games.

Linda L. Griffin

CONTENTS

Foreword   xi

Acknowledgments   xv

Introduction   xvii

Part I. Performance in Team Sports   1

Chapter 1. Classifying, Defining, and Analyzing
Team Sports and Games   3

    The Classification of Sports and Games   3

    The Nature and Definition of Team Sports   6

    Game Play Analysis Models   8

Chapter 2. The Systemic Nature of Team Sports   11

    Exploring Team Sport through Systematic Analysis   11

    Team Sports: Contributions of Systemic Analysis   15

    A French Model of Analysis   18

    Team Sport Modeling   20

Chapter 3. The Internal Logic of Team Sports   23

    The Force Ratio (The Rapport of Strength)   23

    The Competency Network   26

    Tactics and Strategy   27

    Some Principles Underlying Strategy and Tactics   30

Chapter 4. Decision-Making in Team Sports 35

    Configuration of Play 35

    Decision-Making in Sports 38

    Research on Decision-Making and Sports 40

    Elements Involved in Decision-Making 42

    Individual Aspects of Decision-Making 44

    Collective Aspects of Decision-Making 45

Chapter 5. The Player's Tactical Knowledge 49

    The Content of Tactical Knowledge in Invasion
        Team Sports and Games 49

    Action Rules 50

    The Emergence of Action Rules 53

    The Use of Action Rules 54

    Motor Capacities 55

    Principles of Action 56

Chapter 6. The Analysis of Play in Team Sports 59

    Observational Approaches in the Analysis
        of Game Play 60

    Significant Postures and Behaviors 66

    A Frame of Reference for Passing and Shooting 68

Chapter 7. Performance Assessment in Team Sports 73

    Performance Assessment in Team Sports 74

    Facets of Performance Assessment in Team Sports 74

    Current Assessment Practices in Team Sports 75

    Using Numerical Indices for Formative
        Assessment Purposes 78

    Learning to Observe 86

Chapter 8. An Introduction to the Team-Sport
      Assessment Procedure and the Game Performance
      Assessment Instrument   89

    The Team Sport Assessment Procedure (TSAP)   90
    The Game Performance Assessment
      Instrument (GPAI)   94
    Pedagogical Implications   97
    Conclusion   99

Part II. The Teaching-Learning Process in Team Sports   101

Chapter 9. Underlying Theories in the Teaching-Learning
      Process of Games and Sports   103

    A Conception of Apprenticeship   104
    An Observational Approach of the Game Play   107
    A Set of Situations in a Learning Process   110
    The Debate of Ideas—A Teaching Strategy
      for Understanding and Learning in Team Sports   112
    Critical Features of the Debate-of-Ideas   116
    The Connection Between Doing and Understanding   118
    Technical/Tactical Debate   119
    Conclusion   122

Chapter 10. Constructing Team Sport Knowledge   123

    The Learning Process in Team Sports:
      Prior and Current Models   123
    Tactical Decision Learning Model (TDLM)   128
    Making Sense of Learning   129
    Toward the Modeling of Students' Play
      in Team Sports in Secondary School   130
    Transformation   136

Chapter 11. Critical Issues in the Teaching of Team Sports   141

       Common Traits in Games and Sports   141

       Adaptation and Learning in Relation

          to Team Games and Sports   144

       Sport Ethics   152

Chapter 12. Research and Development:

       Working Toward Evidence-Based Practice   155

       Exploring the Development of Learners'

          Game Knowledge   157

       Situated Learning Theory   160

       Implications for Learning and Instruction   163

Bibliography   165

Endnotes   177

Index   179

FOREWORD

As is the case for many physical education teachers, I spent hundreds of hours throughout my childhood, and even more during my adolescence, practicing various sports. In the fifties, playing informal hockey and skating for hours on outside ice rinks was to young Quebecers what playing football or basketball is to many young Americans. Personally, I skated a lot not only on outside ice rinks but also on frozen ponds and frozen parts of the St. Lawrence River. On many occasions, I also played with a hockey stick and a puck, either on skates or on foot. However, despite a reasonably high level of technical skills, I never truly excelled in playing real hockey matches. All the technical ingredients were there, but somehow there was something missing. In retrospect, I must admit that my game presented serious defects in terms of strategy and, even more so, in terms of tactics.

It was only at the university level, in Quebec City, that I was formally taught my first physical education courses as I enrolled in a physical education teaching program. There were many courses focused on the teaching of sports, including individual, dual, or team sports. But every time a particular sport involved playing against one or several opponents, whether it was badminton, tennis, basketball, football, hockey, or volleyball, priority in learning tasks was always given to the technical aspects of the sport involved.

As soon as I completed my bachelor's degree in physical education teaching, I enrolled in a graduate program at the University of Illinois at Urbana-Champaign. There, I was exposed to John Dewey's "Learning by Doing" theory but completed a master's degree in physiology of exercise. I had entered the world of kinesiology, or sports science. Five years later, I returned to the United States and enrolled in a Ph.D. program in educational research and design at Florida State University. One of the leaders in the department where I studied was named Dr. Robert Gagné, who had written, among other books, *The Conditions of Learning*. Understandably, the place was a stronghold of behaviorism applied to teaching. Given my past learning experiences in track and field, gymnastics, and team sports, this teaching perspective suited me perfectly. Throughout the following 15 years, I taught and researched first the measurement of motor skills and then their formative assessment; in doing so, I had to tackle the matter of tactical skills. Progressively, I shifted toward what one might call the "arts and science of physical activity." Nevertheless, the general sport pedagogy paradigm to which I kept referring was still that of a behaviorist and technical approach; moreover, it was in line with the teaching and assessment practices of most physical education teachers with whom I worked.

By the end of the eighties, I had the pleasure of directing the doctoral program of a colleague who was well acquainted with the work of Piaget and who was convinced of the value of a constructivist approach in the teaching of physical education. The various discussions we both had on the subject enhanced my awareness about constructivism, but I still was not convinced. Then in January 1991, I met Jean-Francis Gréhaigne during an AISEP congress in Atlanta. Since then we have discussed, on many occasions, the various aspects of constructivism as it applies to physical education in general and to the learning of team sports in particular. During the same period of time, I was involved with the revision process of two teacher education programs in my own university. One was concerned with general education at the secondary level, and the other was focused on physical education teaching at both the elementary and secondary levels. It was obvious to me that for members of both revision committees, the student remained at the center of the teaching-learning process, the teacher's task being to facilitate rapport between students and the subject matter. Similarly, each student was perceived to be, in some way, in charge of his or her own education. Moreover, one competency sought in each program was *reflexive thought*, that is, the ability to reflect back on previous experiences and to build from them in view of future practices. Such views were clearly in line with pedagogical principles put forward in recent publications from the Quebec Ministry of Education concerning not only public school curricula but teacher education programs as well. Several American research bodies have expressed the same ideas. It has become clear to me that in many countries, several researchers, teacher educators, and education governing bodies favor a constructivist view of learning.

On the other hand, our own research on professional practices in physical education shows that physical education teachers, when teaching team sports, keep presenting their students with technical solutions to be reproduced or tactical principles to be applied rather than technical or tactical problems to be resolved. And yet I do not recall meeting one single P.E. teacher who would refute the idea of putting the student at the center of the teaching-learning process. Hence, there seems to be a gap between the discourse and actual practices. Some of the reasons for that may be the following:

First, a majority of physical education teachers, particularly those who completed their teacher education many years ago, were given a sports education in which they were essentially taught the "do as I do" method. They then proceeded to apply this model in their own professional practice and do not know how to transform their practice for it to be more in accordance with a constructivist approach.

Second, the little time devoted to physical education at school likely bears on pedagogical choices. Physical education teachers, like all teachers, hope for their students to succeed. But given the time that they have at their disposal, they must proceed quickly. So as soon as students experience learning problems, they are said and shown what to do. Implementing a constructivist approach in the classroom requires assessment procedures in which students become active participants. While students observe peers or reflect on past actions, they are not practicing; therefore, according to many teachers, they are not learning.

Finally, many physical education teachers' reservations may originate from a too-narrow and rigid interpretation of the pedagogical implications associated with a constructivist approach. On the one hand, the construction of knowledge by students does not require that they reinvent the wheel every time they encounter a new learning task. On the other hand, even in a constructivist learning environment, there is room for practicing reproductions of solutions to consolidate students' constructions thought to be promising.

Teaching and Learning Team Sports and Games provides physical education teachers and student teachers with a working tool based both on theoretical aspects and practical considerations drawn from field experimentation. Therefore, it provides some answers to the difficulties and reservations discussed above. Beyond the epistemological debate about the transmission or construction of knowledge, this book also discusses the respective contribution of strategic and tactical components and technical aspects with respect to teaching and learning team sports. Of course, it is not a matter of applying the "all or nothing" rule. What is more at stake is determining which aspect will be given priority and a leading role in the learning process. The traditional approach, the one I was exposed to, consisted first in mastering a series of technical skills to be later exploited in game situations; at that time, tactical aspects were then introduced. Strategic aspects, for their part, were rarely considered. In the tactical approach, students engage in real play from the start. The teacher's strategy is to bring them either (a) to understand and apply predetermined tactical principles, which are still a behaviorist, although cognitive, approach or (b) to solve tactical and strategic problems and, therefore, construct new knowledge (a constructivist approach). As students feel the need while in action, appropriate technical skills become part of the learning tasks.

It probably is too soon to determine the outcome of this technical/tactical debate. Some authors completely advocate the tactical approach while other sport pedagogy specialists keep asking for more scientific evidence, arguing that studies conducted so far show conflicting results. Considering all the attention given to the Teaching Games for Understanding (TGfU) model over the last 10 years or so, the publication of this book appears timely. Clearly, the teaching strategies advocated in the following chapters resemble those of TGfU in the sense that tactical knowledge is given priority over technical skills and that much attention is given to the cognitive aspect of learning. Beyond that, readers will see that the book goes one step further, clearly putting the student at the very center of the teaching-learning process and making the student responsible for the construction of his or her knowledge.

According to an old saying, if we give a person a fish to eat, we nourish that person for one day. If we teach someone how to fish, we nourish that person throughout his or her entire lifetime. This is, I believe, what this book is about.

Paul Godbout, Ph.D.
Professor Emeritus
Laval University
Quebec City
Canada

ACKNOWLEDGMENTS

As you are all aware, the accomplishment of a project of this nature is not without great sacrifice. In such a time-consuming endeavour, family and friends are sometimes neglected. We want to thank our families and close friends for their understanding and support throughout the completion of this book.

Because this book required a significant amount of rewriting and translation, we want sincerely to thank Angela Clarke for her linguistic review of the first few versions of this manuscript. Her expertise helped us to establish a cohesive train of thought from one chapter to the next and greatly contributed to the overall clarity of the text. Her assistance with this project is greatly appreciated. We would also like to thank the Routledge Editorial Team for their support and patience with this book project.

Finally, we want to express our gratitude and recognition to our dear friend and colleague Dr. Paul Godbout, who has been the external conscience throughout the completion of this book. Dr. Godbout has been very instrumental in the evolution of this project by providing us his thoughts and opinions pertaining to content. Being himself an expert on this topic, we also want to sincerely thank him for setting the stage of this book by writing the foreword. Thanks again Paul, and in recognition of your contribution, we collectively raise our glasses from our own little part of the world and express a heartfelt "cheers!"

INTRODUCTION

Play is a privileged part of a child's and adolescent's world. From spontaneous play to traditional games to organized sport, games offer multiple avenues for self expression through a physical activity medium. A certain number of rules preside over the way games are played, and these rules are transmitted from generation to generation, which constitutes a society's cultural patrimony. Nevertheless, games and game play possess traits that are common in all societies. Typically, a child's game play can be characterized as being carefree and organized by rules based on his/her own reality. Caillois (1961) confirms that rules are inseparable from play, even more so when they are recognized institutionally.

At the origin of play, there exists a certain liberty that is characterized by distraction and relaxation but also by seriousness. As stated by Wallon (1941), play is an activity that liberates people from their habitual constraints: It is an opportunity to free the sensorimotor side of their persona to explore and express themselves. For Wallon, play is an excellent means to stimulate imagination because it permits not only one's personal development but also one's relationship with others.

From these different characteristics, play consists of a series of actions that are accomplished in a defined time frame and play space, that follow a set of rules, and that are often accompanied by sensations, tension, and jubilation (Huizinga, 1951). Consequently, what are the distinctive traits of play that lead to these feelings and sensations?

First of all, one of the main sensations that can be associated with play is *social adhesion*. Participants often value the feeling of belonging to a group. The second sensation is often linked to *jubilation*, which refers to the feelings of joy that playing a game should bring. As Huizinga (1951) points out, people play, not because it is cumbersome or perceived to be a burden, but because it brings them pleasure. Play can also bring a strong sensation in relation to *fiction*, which doesn't necessarily mean that there is a total escape from all contingencies of daily life. It is merely a pause from certain norms and obligations in the presence of another reality, which presents a different set of constraints and obligations. This reality is *game play*. These three sensations can result in a fourth sensation, which is the development of *immediate interest*. The development of interest through game play can be harnessed through learning and other external motivators such as competition and success.

In a school setting, play is first associated with recess: a short leisure period between two classes. Recess is a time to have fun doing different things that do not necessarily have an immediate goal. In physical education classes, play, and especially game play, is structured and based on specific learning outcomes. Game confrontation between students is often integrated to put into practice what has been learned.

In the past two decades, educational reform movements in many countries have been pointing toward more authentic learning experiences for students across the curriculum, which includes physical education. Sport-related games teaching in physical education provides the primary content that teachers use to attain specific learning outcomes. From a research perspective, there is an ongoing agenda that continues to grapple with the effectiveness of different available teaching strategies. From a practical perspective, several works have addressed how to integrate these strategies in classroom settings; however, most textbooks available today lack details about the theoretical foundations that underlie these different teaching strategies. *Teaching and Learning Team Sports and Games* focuses not only on how to teach sports and games via the use of different teaching strategies but also on the underlying theories which support these strategies.

Written as a resource for teachers (pre and in service) and coaches, *Teaching and Learning Team Sports and Games* is a *theory to practice* textbook that focuses on the foundations and applications of constructivism as applied to the teaching and learning of invasion team sports and games. This textbook retraces the evolution of games teaching from Mahlo (1974) to Deleplace (1979), to Bunker and Thorpe (1982), and it conceptualizes this evolution with respect to the modern theories of constructivism to aid teachers in developing more educational teaching-learning scenarios for their students in relation to invasion sports and games. More precisely, this textbook explores a tactical approach to games teaching beyond the work of Bunker and Thorpe (1982). Bunker and Thorpe proposed a Teaching Games for Understanding (TGfU) model to pose and answer critical questions regarding *what to teach* and *how to teach it* for students to develop a more complete knowledge in relation to the games they play.

Teaching and Learning Team Sports and Games goes beyond TGfU and proposes the Tactical Decision Learning model (TDLM), which is a more in-depth model for the teaching of sports-related games in a school physical education setting. In part 1, performance in team sports is defined, the different elements that influence performance are identified, and the methods to measure and assess performance are explained. In part 2, the focus is on the teaching-learning process itself. In this section, the underlying theories of games teaching and the learning process are thoroughly explained. The major focus of this section is to explore the notion of constructivism and how it can be used in games teaching and learning. Issues surrounding the development of students' critical thinking skills and construction of knowledge will be foregrounded as the different teaching strategies that emphasize tactical learning are examined.

Teaching and Learning Team Sports and Games will benefit pre-service and in-service physical education teachers, coaches involved in youth sports, and teachers in their development as games teachers through the use of a constructivist frame. *Teaching and Learning Team Sports and Games* provides teachers and coaches with a theoretical foundation aimed at improving their interventions (i.e., teaching) in relation to the teaching of invasion team games and sports. This foundation will enable these practitioners to better comprehend games teaching, permitting them to construct and offer more educational learning scenarios to their students.

Throughout this book we have used the terms "student" and "player." In many cases these terms are interchangeable; students often are, or will be, players and vice versa. As used in this book, the terms help situate knowledge about the teaching and learning of games. The use of these terms is not designed to be limiting in any way. Concepts, ideas, and information conveyed for "players" or "students" can be useful in the teaching of games whether the people receiving the information are players on a team or students in a classroom gaining information about physical education.

During a period when the value of physical education is continually questioned, *Teaching and Learning Team Sports and Games* will be an indispensable resource that contains detailed information no other source has yet to offer: a complete and comprehensible textbook on the theoretical foundations and applications of games teaching, which foregrounds a constructivist teaching-learning approach. Furthermore, this book is unique because it brings the perspectives and expertise of three individuals from three different cultures to a topic that is of interest to physical education teachers and coaches around the world.

I

Performance in Team Sports

1

CLASSIFYING, DEFINING, AND ANALYZING TEAM SPORTS AND GAMES

In this first chapter, we provide an overview of a classification system for games. We will specifically focus on team sports that are classified as invasion games and present different models for analyzing game play.

THE CLASSIFICATION OF SPORTS AND GAMES

Logic, tactics, and practice are three notions that involve two associated ideas: a) the reality concerning game play is intelligible; and b) the intervention in relation to this reality can be the subject of objective, rational inquiry. As several authors have stated, game play is essentially a player's personal property (ownership) (Deleplace, 1995; Wade, 1970). This idea emphasizes that through time, players have had a major influence on the evolution of game play because they are the ones actually applying game play concepts in practical contexts. Coaches, referees, and rules of play are also factors that influence game play.

Through time, the dynamics of game play and the essence of team sports and games prompt players to better use the potentialities reflected in the spirit of fundamental rules (Deleplace, 1966) or primary rules (Almond, 1986a). Deleplace (1979) considers that the traditional technical analysis model must be contextualized within actual game situations in which a "force ratio" between opponents is present. Hence, this tactical analysis model's primary function is to identify the different

possible game configurations within this force ratio and also to identify the pertinent indices that characterize them. Second, this model
consists of extracting the principles that lead to a configuration's
transformation. The extraction of these principles permits one access
to the internal logic of a particular sport or game. This internal logic
is the product of the game's continuous interaction between the
game's main rules and the changing game responses produced by
players.

The fundamental or primary rules are concerned with the means to
an end, and to achieve the end by other means is not playing the game.
Thus, primary rules supply the game with its essential character. Primary
rules are what makes basketball, "basketball" not volleyball (Almond,
1986a).

Fundamental rules have a major influence on the relationship
between opponents because they determine certain parameters in
which players must function. A particular game or sport is organized
around a nucleus of fundamental and complementary rules that
evolve to try and adapt to the changes introduced by new techniques
and tactics while still conserving the essence or "spirit" of that particular game or sport. These fundamental or primary rules are characterized by:

- *The modalities of scoring*, which relate to the particular characteristics of the game's target and the necessary skills involved in
  order to score.
- *The players' rights* (both from an offensive and defensive standpoint), which are based upon the modalities of scoring that complete those rights with respect to the equality of chances.
- *The liberty of action* that players have with the ball to give the
  game a specific character.
- *The modalities of physical engagement* that ensure the respect of
  the three previous rules.

The knowledge of rules within their specific logic is necessary to better understand the logic of observed game play behaviors, both technical and tactical. According to Almond in the book *Rethinking
Teaching Games* (1986b), games can be classified in the following
four categories: invasion, fielding/runscoring, net/wall, and target
games.

For his part, Gréhaigne (1989) adds another dimension to the classification of invasion games. He specifies that the target in invasion games

Invasion Games

1. Handball
   Basketball
   Netball
   Team handball
   Korkball
   Tchouk-ball
   Ultimate frisbee
   Waterpolo

   American football
   Soccer
   Rugby
   Gaelic football
   Australian football
   Hurling/Camogie
   Speedball
   Touchball (Finnish rugby)

   Stick-ball
   Field hockey
   Lacrosse
   Cycle polo
   Shinty
   Roller hockey
   Ice hockey

2. Games can have:
   a) either a focused target, like hockey.
   b) or an open-ended target, like football.

Fielding/Runscoring
Baseball
Softball
Rounders
Cricket
Kick Ball (football cricket)

Net/Wall

Net/Racquet	**Net/hand**	**Wall**
Badminton	Volleyball	Squash
Tennis		Handball (court)
Table Tennis		Paddle Ball
Paddle Tennis		Raquetball
Platform Tennis		Basque pelote

Target Games

Golf	Ten (or 5 or 9) Pin	
Croquet	Duckpin	
Curling	Pub skittles	
Pool	Billiards	
	Snooker	

can greatly influence their particular characteristics. Typically, targets can be vertical or horizontal, big or small, high or low, and within the playing area or at its extremity. These characteristics can have different effects on the technical and tactical components of the game. He adds that games can also be characterized by being played either on a bigger or smaller playing surface. Finally, Gréhaigne mentions that the way players interact with the projectile can also define games. The interaction is a factor that either reunites or separates opponents as they fight to gain possession of the projectile.

THE NATURE AND DEFINITION OF TEAM SPORTS

Figure 1.1 illustrates the continuous and fundamentally reversible character of play. In a natural sequence of events in any invasion game, players are either defenders or attackers in connection with the configurations of play. One can note that we differenciate between the notions of "attack" and "offense". The offensive aspect of the attack is scoring or taking a shot on a goal. Conservation of the ball is the defensive aspect of the attack, especially when the ball circulates at the rear of the effective play-space. Recovering the ball or putting pressure on the opposing team to regain possession of the ball is the offensive aspect of the defense. Defending one's goal consists in the defensive aspect of the defense. We have already moved from a simple attack-defense model to a more complex model with the use of offensive and defensive notions.

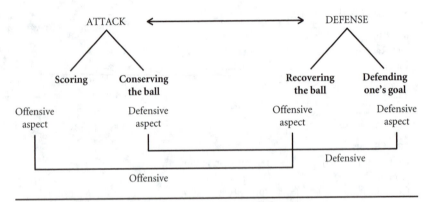

Fig. 1.1 Concepts related to the notion of opposition (translation from Gréhaigne, 1989).

As we examine a little closer, team sports offer certain closely interwoven characteristics within a given set of rules, focused toward winning the match (Gréhaigne, 1989, 1992; Gréhaigne & Godbout, 1995). These characteristics are:

- **A force ratio.** A group of players confronts another group of players, fighting for or exchanging an object (most often a ball)
- **A choice of motor skills.** Mastery of a certain range of motor responses—those of daily life or others that are much more specific and elaborate

- **Individual and collective strategies.** Implicit or explicit decisions, taken by the group, on the basis of a common frame of reference to defeat the opponents

The emphasis put on the inseparable character of the relationship among these three elements has consequences on the way one approaches or patterns team sports (Gréhaigne, 1994). The main challenge of team sports according to Deleplace (1979) is that in an *opposition relationship*, each of two teams must coordinate its actions to recover, conserve, and move the ball so as to bring it into the scoring zone and score.

Team sports are defined by Gréhaigne & Roche (1990) as the self-organization of a group confronted by another group with antagonistic interests. To score and prevent scoring players use common strategies:

1. To resolve anticipation-coincidence motor problems, that is, the preparation of responses before the arrival of the ball and the regulation of these responses as the ball arrives
2. To make informed choices among potential answers depending upon likely costs and benefits
3. To manage the varying courses of the players and the trajectories of the ball in urgent conditions of decision making

Brackenridge (1979) proposes a struggle for territorial dominance within a set of rules or structural parameters that includes significant cognition and technical aspects and in which coincidence-anticipation is paramount. The struggle for territorial dominance is decided by a system of scoring, which determines victory. The code of rules identifies the problems surrounding the achievement of territorial dominance and ensures that both teams or individuals meet and compete on equal and fair grounds. Gréhaigne (1992) indicates that this way of viewing team sports brings in three main categories of problems:

- **Problems related to space and time.** In an attack situation, one must find solutions to problems of individual and collective handling of the ball to overtake, use, or avoid varying mobile obstacles. In a defense mode, one must bring forward obstacles to slow down or stop the forward progression of the ball and of the opponents in view of an eventual recapture of the ball.
- **Problems related to information.** Players must also deal with problems related to the production of uncertainty for the opponents and of certainty for their partners in a situation that remains

fundamentally reversible. The reduction of uncertainty for the team in possession of the ball is a function of the quality of the communication codes and the choice of explicit tactics, thus allowing appropriate choices, understood by all teammates, according to momentary configurations of play.

- **Problems related to organization.** Players must accept the switch from an individual to a collective project. Each player must truly merge the collective project with their personal actions while giving the best of themselves to the group.

Generally, in team sports the main organization for a team is its "system of play." It is defined as

"The general form in which players' offensive and defensive actions are organized by establishing a precise arrangement of certains tasks in relation to positions and field coverage and certain principles of cooperation among them. The system of play is the basic structure of collective team tactics." (Teodorescu, 1965)

In the following section, we will share different game play analysis models with the goal of situating the conceptions and limitations related to teaching team sports and games.

GAME PLAY ANALYSIS MODELS

In this section, we present three different analysis models based on two reference frameworks: one based on pedagogical conceptions and the other based on the learner's conceptions.

Analytical Model

Traditional conceptions of a team's strength hold that it is equal to the sum of the individuals that make it up. We juxtapose quality individuals to make up a team. Game play is decomposed into simple elements that, when combined with quality players, result in a quality or high performance.

Pedagogical Conceptions of the Analytical Model The analytical model is heavily influenced by rational and mechanical theories. This approach analyzes game components (technical skills) outside the actual game context. Game components that are decomposed and analyzed individually are then associated with each other. Within this approach, which is based on a behavioral teaching approach, a major importance is attributed to imitation and repetition. However, it has often been noted that imitation and repetition is accomplished in a near-total absence of creative or critical thinking.

Structuralist Model

In contrast to the previous model, the team is perceived to be more than the sum of the individuals who compose it. The team is seen as a structured group of individuals or a "social microsystem" working together toward a common goal (Teodorescu, 1965). Within this microsystem, there exists a reciprocal coordination of individual and collective actions from which the group tries to draw general principles to better understand the game.

Pedagogical Conceptions of the Stucturalist Model The structuralist model relies on different factors of execution, such as speed, strength, and power, to develop team play. Its main goal is to organize team strategies and tactics through practice situations that put emphasis on ball circulation and player movement. These strategies and tactics are modeled in practice and then tried in actual matches. Game behaviors and actions are deduced from game situations, thus producing a wider array of possibilities and reflecting the different realities within a particular game or sport.

Systemic Model

In the two previous models, analysis of game play has focused on players of a same team without taking into consideration what actions the opposing team could be developing at the same moment. In the systemic model, there is a switch in the pedagogical focus because its aim is to explain game play from the oppositional relationship that constantly exists between two opposing teams. By looking at games through the analysis of the force ratio between opponents, one considers a game's reality in its entirety.

Pedagogical Conceptions of the Systemic Model When using this particular approach to analyze games, the focus is on trying to explain the oppositional relationship to develop better understanding of the game and to better execute actions during the game. Different aspects of game performance must be analyzed within this model, such as a player's combativeness in one-on-one confrontation, cognitive work, and the identification and comprehension of game play principles. Also, the perceptual elements of game play must be developed for a player to be able to apply them in the anticipation of future game situations.

Playing is a very important aspect of learning how to play. One of the major goals of games during childhood is to provide an outlet where the child can affirm him/herself in a context of self-actualization. A teacher or coach offers children game situations that permit them to satisfy their own desires and not the ones created by adults (teachers, coaches, parents, etc.). Essentially, the idea is to place the child in a game situation that is adapted to be relevant to different age and developmental levels. Thus the educator's challenge is to find or imagine situations that present players with challenges that must include a force ratio between opposing teams.

In conclusion, it is noteworthy that the systemic analysis model will provide the foundation and framework in which our exploration and explanation of teaching team games and sports will be based.

2

THE SYSTEMIC NATURE OF TEAM SPORTS

To better understand the principles at work in team sports, a pertinent approach could be to model the interactions between the players and the environment as a complex system. In team sports, environmental variables represent fluctuating conditions that momentarily constrain the organization of players' actions (Ali & Farraly, 1990; Bouthier, 1989; Caron & Pelchat, 1975; David, 1993; Davids, Hanford, & Williams, 1994; Gréhaigne, 1988; Gréhaigne & Godbout, 1995; Walliser, 1977). For example, according to the available space, the ball carrier's choices will dictate the success of an attack. In order to better understand such choices, this chapter examines, in the first part, the systemic nature of team sport. The second part presents a French analysis model based on the oppositional relationship.

EXPLORING TEAM SPORT THROUGH SYSTEMIC ANALYSIS

Since invasion team sports represent the interaction of two separate entities, it is essential to explore the analysis of these interactive systems through the various sub-disciplines (e.g., motor learning). Our study of team sport from a systemic point of view will center on the theory of dynamic systems.

Theory of Dynamic Systems

Systemic analysis was born in the last 30 years as a result of the union of various disciplines such as biology, information theory, cybernetics, and systems theory. According to Atlan (1979; 1992), it should not be considered a science, a theory, or a discipline but rather a new process allowing for the gathering and organization of knowledge in view of more efficient action. According to Walliser (1977), the systemic approach aims to find answers to three essential concerns:

1. The drive to come back (as a reaction to ultra-analytic tendencies of some sciences) to a more synthetic approach that would recognize properties of dynamic interactions between elements of a whole, giving it a totality of character.
2. The need, in order to conceive and control large and complex wholes, to put together a method that would make it possible to obtain and organize knowledge so as to better relate means and objectives.
3. The necessity, in face of fragmentation and the dispersal of knowledge, to promote a utilitarian language that could support the articulation and integration of theoretical models and methodological precepts scattered in various disciplines.

General Properties of Systems The analytical approach tries to break down a system to its simplest constituent elements. Then, modifying one variable at a time, it tries to deduce general laws that make it possible to predict the properties of the system in different conditions. For such predictions to be feasible, additive laws of elementary properties must come into play. However, in the case of highly complex systems, such as a soccer match, these additive laws do not work. Therefore, such systems must be approached with new methods, such as those gathered under the systemic approach. Studying a system's behavior over time leads to the determination of action rules that are used to influence or modify the state of the system.

A systemic approach relies on the notion of system or a whole made up of interacting elements. These elements include:

1. A whole in reciprocal rapport with an environment, whereby such exchanges provide the whole with some autonomy
2. A whole composed of interacting subsystems, such that interdependence ensures a certain coherence
3. A whole submitted to more or less important modifications over time while maintaining a basic permanence

Often in a classical approach, the only explanation of phenomena relies on linear causality; it is an explanatory mode based on a logical chain of causes and effects. With the systemic approach, movement replaces permanence, flexibility replaces inflexibility, and adaptability replaces stability. Notions of flow and flow balance join those of force and force balance. Hence, by integrating time, a systemic approach reveals the interdependence of phenomena and their gradual change. Causality has become circular and is now conceived of as a regulation loop (Bertalanffy, 1972; Caverni, 1988; Caverni, Bastien, Mendelsohn, & Tiberghien, 1988; Morin, 1986; Rosnay, 1975).

Two main categories of systems are defined: closed systems and open systems. A closed system exchanges neither energy nor matter with its environment; it is self-sufficient. On the other hand, an open system relates constantly with its environment. It exchanges energy, matter, and information useful for maintaining its organization. Its complexity takes into account variety and interaction between elements. Some liaisons may be studied either from a causal point of view (balance, stability, etc.) or from an end product point of view (adaptation and learning).

Systems and Subsystems A system is said to be quasidecomposable if it can be decomposed into semi-isolated subsystems, with some interaction between them and the environment (Walliser, 1977). With reference to a given system, one may consider the following in the context of team sports:

1. *Microsystems*, which are obtained by retaining only a few subsystems with all their interactions. For example, the confrontation between two teams at a given time, each possessing its own configuration of play.
2. *Infrasystems*, which represent few subsystems with some of their interactions (that is, 1 vs. 1 or 2 vs. 2) at some point in the match.

As was the case for general characteristics of systems, interactions between subsystems are energy based or information based. These subsystems may organize themselves into various types of networks, either superimposed upon or merged inside the system. Each subsystem in turn can generally be decomposed into other subsystems according to an interlocking order that reflects hierarchies or multiple sets of combinations. Relationships among elements of a given level differ in terms of nature and intensity from those among elements of subsystems pertaining to different levels. For example, one may not switch from 5 vs. 5 soccer to 11 vs. 11 without reorganizing one's knowledge and capacities. This situation is true even though relatively homogeneous subsystems may sometimes show up, as, for example, a three-player configuration of play at the periphery of the field between a defender, a midfield player, and the involved wing.

Systems and Time The temporal dimension is important for studying systems because it is the medium through which they operate and evolve. All things considered, nothing may be fundamentally understood about soccer if one does not shift from a spatial to a temporal reference system while processing information. The synchronous properties of a system relate to the relationships among various characteristics of that system at a given time. The diachronic properties relate to the relationships of those same characteristics through many successive moments in time. They make it possible to bring to light the system's evolutionary trends. In a quasidecomposable system, one may differentiate among modifications mainly related to the system's structure, functioning, evolution, or relationships to these three phenomena. The system's structure, in a strict sense, rests upon the whole set of its most unvarying characteristics; thus, the system's structure ensures its very existence and its permanence. In a larger sense, the structure is formed by all the system's characteristics at a given point in time, thus reflecting the state of the system at that moment. The system's functioning relates on the one hand to each subsystem's transformations and, on the other hand, to flows passing through linking channels between subsystems and between the system and its environment. The system's evolution is brought about, on the one hand, by a change in the subsystems' transformation laws and, on the other hand, by changes in the way the system organizes itself into subsystems and changes in the linking channels between the system and the environment.

For instance, in soccer, the structural dimension is characterized by:

1. A boundary that establishes the frontiers of the system (i.e. the play area)
2. Elements that may be counted and grouped into categories, such as the players, the attackers or defenders, the ball, and so on
3. "Containers" in which energy or information is stocked (the potentialities within a certain play configuration, the goalkeeper, players' energy potential, etc.)
4. A communication network that allows energy and information exchanges (the rules, the code of play, a common frame of reference to read and interpret plays in the same way, etc.)

The functional dimension is characterized by:

1. Flows of energy, information, or various elements that include players, the ball, replacements, state of fatigue, and so on
2. Gates controlling the rate of various flows, such the play leader, players' momentary tactical choices, the referee, rules of play, and so on

3. Delays resulting from flows moving at different speeds or from the gate response time, as in situations of creating open space, gaining an interval, restoring a defensive block, and so on
4. Regulation loops, either proactive or reactive, that play a large part in the system's behavior by managing all parameters, either taking information to adjust the game plan, setting a defensive reserve, or modifying the system of play.

Regulation: General Principle The information process uses a collection mechanism and makes use of information to modify the system. To characterize this process, one may consider five types of activity that intervene, in a cyclic way, in its functioning (see Mahlo, 1974).

- **Information activity.** Translating action into a conceptual form of observed real phenomena (perception)
- **Prospecting activity.** Constructing probable, possible, or desirable schemes about the future (planning)
- **Decision activity.** Translating intents and aspirations into actions on reality (programming and management)
- **Execution activity.** Transforming the system through voluntary and coordinated actions (execution)
- **Control activity.** Collecting information about the results of actions with a view to pursuing or transforming the current action or the upcoming one (regulation)

TEAM SPORTS: CONTRIBUTIONS OF SYSTEMIC ANALYSIS

To obtain more information about the structure and function of play, we will use a systemic approach, as presented in chapter 1, to discuss the modeling of team sports.

Some Concepts Related to the Notion of Opposition

In a soccer match or any other type of invasion game, structures and configurations of play should be considered as a whole, rather than be examined piece by piece. Systems with many dynamically interacting elements are capable of rich and varied patterns of behavior that are clearly different from the behavior of each component considered separately. The influence of general systems theory is now clearly evident, and one must analyze the performances of the players as a system in synergy with the environment.

Indeed, in a match, the opposition generates the unexpected, and there is a constant need to adapt to constraints brought about by the confrontation. A match rarely relies upon the simple application of schematics learned during practice sessions. Thus, most often during the game, one can foresee only probabilities of evolution for the attack and defense configurations; hence the importance of heuristics to quickly solve the problems inherent in specific interactions between two teams.

In a classic learning approach, one tries before anything else to teach students technical skills and to maintain order on the playing field by, for example, the use of formal groupings. However, it could be argued that it is just as important, and maybe even more so, to get the players to optimally manage disorder (Villepreux, 1987; Gréhaigne, 1989; 1992a). This type of approach, which puts forward "opposition" and "disorder management" as a base for any progress, brings to light new concepts that appear fundamental for a renewal of team sport teaching. Figure 2.1 identifies some concepts that come into focus when one points out opposition as a fundamental element of the modeling process in team sports.

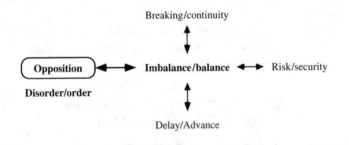

Fig. 2.1 Concepts related to the notion of opposition (translation from Gréhaigne, 1992).

The central notion of opposition leads us to consider the two teams as interacting organized systems. The structural characteristics of these systems consist of a program that can be modified according to acquired experience; their main functional property is learning. The operational conditions of such systems in team sports require that one manage disorder before anything else, while preserving a certain order and thus allowing decisions in a not completely *a priori*, foreseeable environment.

For instance, let us analyze a match, looking at its structural and functional characteristics. By structural, we mean the spatial organization of the constituent synchronic and topological elements of the system, while the functional aspect refers to the various time related processes such as exchanges, regulations, and reorganization of the elements, both the diachronic and kinetic properties.

In a match, from a structural point of view, the elements of the system are represented by the two opposing teams, and the communication network between the two is defined by the rules of the sport. At this level, the idea is to characterize, from a spatial standpoint, the opposition rapport and to analyze the relationships between the strong points of the attack system and those of the defensive system. Notions at stake here are "in block," "in pursuit," center of gravity, circulation of the ball, and so on (Gréhaigne, 1992b; Bouthier, David, & Eloi, 1994; Gréhaigne & Bouthier, 1994). From a functional point of view, one is dealing with the evolution in time of the opposing relationship between the two teams (advance, delay; breaking, continuity; etc.). In this case, each match provides phenomenological data—something original and unique—thus reducing the efficiency of ready-made motor or strategic solutions.

The Consequences

A match constitutes a complex system. Analysis of the game reveals the existence of a large number of interacting variables. On the playing surface, a nonhomogenous distribution of the players brings about a nonhomogeneous distribution of the energy state of the players. A certain type of homogeneous scattering characterizes the equilibrium state toward which invasion team sports systems always evolve. It corresponds, therefore, to homogeneity of the players' distribution on the different energetic states. The degree of homogeneity of the configurations of play can also be explained by the probabilities of the presence of the players at certain areas of the playing surface.

Another way to show the homogeneity of a system consists in defining the microstates of the system of attack and defense. Each microstate is defined by a distribution of the players on the playing surface's area according to their positions, orientations, and speeds. One can call this type of distribution a *dynamic configuration of play*. The apparent disorder indicates a more general homogeneity than the simple spatial distribution of the players on the ground because the latter distribution influences only two energy levels: potential and speed. In those situations of opposition, the kinetic interactions lead to the stabilization of the spatially nonhomogeneous states by other nonhomogeneous distributions, which appear homogenous if one looks for certain energetic states. It means that those states would seem to be more homogeneous for an observer who would be able to recognize the different kinetic states. Conversely, a classic observation would stress the heterogeneous aspects by dealing only with positions and geometric shapes. In our opinion, that is how the dialectic equilibrium/disequilibrium of the game operates. On the one hand, very stable structures make one think of a crystalline structure, defined as rigid and with few chances of evolution, as for example in set-plays. On the other hand, the dynamic configurations of play have within themselves a number of transformations limited according to the different possibilities of the continuous evolution of the game but nevertheless important if one chooses a break in modifying the movement during its process.

This group of elements forms a foundation for our framework of analysis. Dynamic systems are able to attain multiple patterns of stability in achieving a state of coordination with the opposition. A theoretical framework that focuses on the achievement of coordination within a dynamic system may be appropriate for the study of configurations of play.

A FRENCH MODEL OF ANALYSIS

In this section, we are going to present the Deleplace model, the tactical matrix of technique and team sport modeling.

The practice modeling presented in Deleplace's work (1966; 1979) gave birth to the school of "tactical approach" (Bouthier, 1984; Deleplace, 1992). These authors have demonstrated that the intervention of cognitive processes is decisive for the advanced organization of play and the control of motor responses (Bouthier, 1986). Their advocates hypothesize that this approach yields better results than two other pedagogical methods. One method, "the execution model approach," focuses on the player's repetition of efficient solutions produced by experts, while the other, "the self adaptive model approach," postulates that judicious variations in the setting are the most efficient for players to discover solutions and develop skills. The central strategy of the tactical approach calls for the presentation of essential information concerning the tactical advance and organization of actions during game play and then for the actual implementation of such actions in relatively self-sustaining and tactics-oriented patterns of play. These patterns, borrowed from actual game play, are not to be confounded with traditional drills. They are selected because they can be played out independently of a match situation, that they call for tactical decisions, and that the outcome remains open-ended.

Nevertheless, the amount of information provided to the player must remain limited, and it is the quality of the information that is determining. In that respect, prior analysis of the internal logic of the sport by a coach, a teacher, or some other expert provides useful data. Based on such analyses, one can draw the player's attention to typical patterns of play. This way, under time constraints, the player has at his or her disposal an already-worked-out mental picture for solving the problem at hand.

Thus, the tactical approach to team sports focuses on players' exploration of the various possibilities of game play and of their modeling based on defensive and offensive matrices. If one looks carefully, the internal logic of every team sport refers to a coherent system of representation—the matrices. In a general sense, a matrix, according to the *Oxford English Dictionary*, is a "place where something begins or develops." In this particular context, in a more figurative sense, the matrix is a shared frame of reference that makes it possible for players to interpret or even anticipate the general movement of the unfolding play. It constitutes a common origin of knowledge and responses for players. The defensive matrix, whatever its shape, deployment, or successive new developments, is at the same time the simplest and the most general matrix that will make it possible to counter the offensive movement attempted by the opponent in possession of the ball. For its part, the offensive matrix is first and foremost the choice of a way of penetrating into the defensive system, given its momentary configuration. Thus, in an invasion game such as soccer, as illustrated in Figure 2.2, the principle of the defensive matrix, which consists in circulating between the various defense lines in order to oppose attackers, is paired, for its offensive counterpart, with the principle of transformation of the initiated movement to maintain one's advance on the defensive replacement. At this moment, the notion of double-impact organization becomes very important because it emphasizes the immediacy of switching from attacker to defender in the event of losing possession of the ball.

Fig. 2.2 Relationship between technique, tactics, and athletic potential.

What is the connection between tactics and technique? The model presented in Figure 2.2 highlights the interdependent nature of tactics, technique, and athletic potential. The player also devises action plans in accord with strategic decisions and makes adjustments as effective action proceeds.

Any decision with regard to the context and theory of play becomes valid only if it can be efficiently translated into action. This implies that a player actually has at his or her disposal a range of corresponding responses (i.e., individual or collective technical skills). Although tactics make up the context that justifies technical skills, these skills should not be considered as secondary. Techniques constitute the tools for the execution of tactics (Mahlo, 1974). Thus, the educational setting should not oppose technical learning and tactical learning but rather should articulate them in a tactical matrix of technique.

It is well known that the motor execution of a tactical choice requires physical energy. Indeed, fatigue not only affects the quality of skill execution but also affects the lucidity of choices. Thus, athletic potential is another limitation factor for the activity.

TEAM SPORT MODELING

The task of a team sport player lies in the ability to detect, during game play, the incipient evolutions in the oppositional relationship. The player must infer or deduct the choices of appropriate successive actions for both offensive and defensive purposes to possible game situations that can develop on the playing surface at any moment.

The shape of a particular game play configuration, like the orientation of offensive or defensive action, has sense according to the characteristics of evolving action from the opposing team. In an offensive situation, the offensive team must consider the state of the defenders' movements and actions, both individually and collectively. In a defensive situation, the defenders must consider the state of the attackers' movements and actions, both individually and collectively. Understanding these reciprocal relationships between the states of movement on the two faces of the opposition and knowing how they operate in real game play constitutes, by definition, *tactical intelligence* in actual game play. At all levels of play, the problem is to reach an automated state of conscious-centered activity.

The reality of evolving game play presents a great multiplicity of different concrete game situations. One can say that there are practically never two game situations that are absolutely identical. Hence, it is almost impossible to re-create all of these situations during practice sessions, but if we consider their characteristics, they can be categorized to form patterns with a small number of categories or types of situations that constitute so many separable tactical units. For each of these units, it becomes possible to explain the foreseeable evolution in the particular oppositional relationship that characterizes it. This explanation constitutes what we can call the law of evolution of play in accordance with a particular tactical unit.

In constructing a model, the problem is therefore to reduce the whole complexity of the game to the smallest number of elements, articulated to a highly logical functional unit. On one hand, the player develops a clearly understood functional logic of game play; on the other hand, he or she understands that particular aspects depend on his or her perceptual-motor skills. In chapter 3 we will use the model and concepts present in this chapter to expand our focus on the internal logic of team sports.

3

THE INTERNAL LOGIC OF TEAM SPORTS

In relation to team sports, one can consider four notions that are central to the topic of this chapter: *opposition* to opponents, *cooperation* with teammates, *attack* on the opposing team's camp, and *defense* of one's own camp. Each of these four elements comes into play, however the complexity of each interaction may vary depending upon the category of sport involved (Almond, 1986b; Werner, 1989). For instance, in baseball, a fielding/run scoring type of team sport, attack and defense are two separate phases in a given inning while in invasion games, the four elements are at play simultaneously. The basic idea is for each player to cooperate with teammates to better oppose the opponents either while attacking (keeping one's defense in mind) or while defending (getting ready to attack) (Gréhaigne, Godbout, & Bouthier, 1997). Given that two teams play in opposition, a systemic view of team sports brings us to consider two main organizational levels: the *match*, related to the force ratio, and the *team*, related to the competency network.

THE FORCE RATIO (THE RAPPORT OF STRENGTH)

In invasion games, the internal logic of play has its source in the opposition relationship that generates, during each sequence of play, a dynamic of moving from one target to the other. We call this opposition relationship the *force ratio*. It refers to the "antagonist links existing between several players or groups of players confronted by virtue of certain rules of a game that determine a pattern of interaction" (Gréhaigne et al., 1997, p. 516). In all instances, the possession of the ball can change and the direction of play inverts. This fact imposes on both teams an organization whereby an answer to the reversibility comprises location and replacement of general movement generated by the opposition in relation to the depth of the playing surface (Gréhaigne, Bouthier, & David, 1997).

In this general movement, the ball carrier is faced with two interrelated decisions of play:

1. The first is centered around two possibilities: to go directly to the target to shoot or to move the ball closer to the target;
2. The second is linked to the rapport between the width of the playing surface and the number of players that each team can use in the specific part of the playing surface where the play is unfolding at that particular moment. This creates, the alternative of running or passing on one side or the other. The movements are in relation to the width of the playing surface in order to bypass coming opponents.

The target-oriented dynamics, which entail various shapes of movement or shooting according to the available depth and to the widthwise orientation of the play, constitute the essence or "soul" of play. This holds true whatever the particular structure of a sport that determines its primary rules; that is how the game is played and how winning can be achieved (Almond, 1986a), regardless of the surface of play or the characteristics of the targets. The potential for reversibility of general movement at any instance, either in depth or width, is a major characteristic of the internal logic of the force ratio. All players must be aware of their orginal frame of reference (i.e., starting point; home base). At the same time, all players must be capable of initiatives that each teammate can decode to react accordingly or can even anticipate. This double dimension of a collective frame of reference strongly linked to individual initiative is fundamental in team sports however, this aspect is often overlooked.

Different organizational levels can be identified. In fact, during a game, the global opposition relationship that we call "organizational level match" breaks down into partial opposition relationships. These opposition settings that momentarily involve a few players generate a particular shape of play representing the "organizational level partial forefront" (see Figure 3.1). At any moment of the match, this partial forefront contains a third-level opposition unit that links the ball carrier and his or her direct opponent. This is called a "primary organizational level" (Gréhaigne, 1992a).

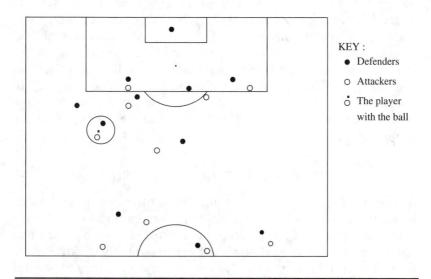

Fig. 3.1 Match, partial forefront, and primary organizational levels. Reprinted, by permission, from Gréhaigne, Godbout, and Bouthier, 1997, pp. 500–516.

Figure 3.1 illustrates the last two organizational levels, whereas the representation of the whole field would show the "organizational level match." Thus the force ratio may be looked at as involving two teams, two sub-groups of players, or eventually two specific players. The continuity of opposition influences the opponents' movements not only at the one-to-one level, but at the partial forefront level and at the match level as well. These simultaneous interlocked opposition settings constitute the context of play (Deleplace, 1979). They evolve in reciprocal rapport in response to the evolution of any part of the system. At any specific moment, according to the evolution of play, this reciprocity relationship offers, for example, a specific problem to attackers but, at the same time, contains pertinent solutions for conducting the action. The solutions are:

- To continue the action at the one-to-one level
- To pursue the attack with the help of partners in the partial forefront
- To change general movement by transforming its shape, its orientation, or even both.

Thus the continual reciprocity relationship between the three organizational levels constitutes the second major characteristic of the internal logic of the force ratio (Deleplace, 1966). As one can see, the general dynamics of team sports can be expressed as a force ratio where, in a sense, two networks of forces are confronting one another. This implies the consideration of a second frame of analysis, that of the "organizational level team" (Gréhaigne & Godbout, 1995). If we consider only one team, we are dealing with the evolution in time of the players' distribution on the players' field or action zone and of the communication network used with regard to the conditions of the confrontation.

THE COMPETENCY NETWORK

At the "organizational level team," the numerous interrelations between players within the team make up what one might call a *competency network* (Gréhaigne, 1992b). Although based on each player's recognized strengths and weaknesses with reference to the practice of the sport, and also on the group's dynamism, the competency network is more a dynamic concept than a static one. The concept of a competency network refers, in general, to the student's game-related behaviors that one can identify in connection with the force ratio between the two participating teams, or with each player's functions within the team. Such behaviors vary depending upon players, moments, external factors, and the particular team sport involved. During play, in connection with behaviors, the notion of *role* is essential for analyzing the competency network. In this case, *role* refers to behaviors that convey what a player thinks he or she ought to do, given the way he or she experiences the rapport of forces or the competency network within the team, and how the player manages his or her resources in a system of constraints.

The function within the group, chosen by the player or assigned by the teacher or by the group, is another indicator of the player's position in the team's dynamics. At the interface of the player's logic, the team's logic, and the internal logic of the sport involved, the player's function in this competency network often is a reliable indicator of the reciprocal rapport between the player and the team. Contrary to what one might think, cooperation in team sports, as in other aspects of life, goes far beyond simple goodwill. For the competency network to be efficient, there is a need for both effort and restraint on the part of many players if not all of them.

In conclusion, from a systemic point of view, one could consider a team sport as the functioning of two competency networks involved in a force ratio. It should then be clear that the very existence of both the force ratio between opponents and of the competency network within each team makes it necessary for each team to try to anticipate the opponents' attacks and defenses and plan according to its offensive and defensive actions. It also becomes useful for each team and player to reflect upon the efficacy of decisions made during the encounter itself, depending upon one's partners' or opponents' behaviors. For this reason, it appears necessary to explore the notions of tactics and strategy.

TACTICS AND STRATEGY

Although found in a completely different context, the terms *strategy* and *tactics* have been used for a long time in the vocabulary of war. According to Von Clausewitz (1989) the strategist determines for the whole act of war a goal corresponding to the object of war. He sets up a war design compatible with the resources of the state, elaborates the plan of the different campaigns, organizes the engagements of each of them, and combines the actions of the military forces and organizes them into systems to preserve their coherence. Von Clausewitz adds that for the strategist, any conflict calls into play physical, mental, and moral factors. The problem then consists in maintaining reflection or theory at the center of these three tendencies as if suspended among three attracting forces or magnets. For his part, the tactician focuses on a more limited, concrete, and generally geographic objective, adapted to the strategic plans. The tactician conducts the battle or operation in sight by adapting the action, combining maneuvers, and deciding on the engagement of the different means of combat. Von Clausewitz points out the relative subordination of the latter to the former: The strategist takes time into account and accompanies the tactician on the field.

Similarly, the European school of team sports makes a distinction between strategy and tactics. For Bouthier (1988), strategy refers to all plans, principles of play, and action guidelines decided upon before a match to organize the activity of the team and the players during the game. The finalized strategy may either concern the most important general options of play or specify the intervention of players for different categories of play. For their part, tactics involve all orientation operations voluntarily executed during the game by the players to adapt to the immediate requirements of an ever-changing opposition, their spontaneous actions, or those organized through the predetermined strategy. Similarly, for Gréhaigne and Godbout (1995) strategy refers to:

> ...these elements discussed in advance in order for the team to organize itself. Tactics are a punctual adaptation to new configurations of play and to the circulation of the ball; they are therefore an adaptation to opposition. As discussed by Gréhaigne (1994) strategy concerns (a) the general order, that is, the outside order form resulting from the general strategic choices of the team (background play, team composition...), and (b) the positions to be covered according to particular instructions each player receives in training (assigned position). For their part, tactics relate to (a) the positions taken in reaction to an adversary in a game situation (effective position) and (b) the adaptation of the team to the conditions of play (flexibility). (p. 491)

There is a fundamental difference between strategy and tactics as far as their relationship with time is concerned. Strategy is associated with more elaborate cognitive processes because the decisions made are based on reflection without time constraints. Tactics operate under strong time constraints. During the learning process, one can use both strategic and tactical aspects of the game whenever temporal pressure is reduced. During regular play, tactics are of paramount importance for players near the ball defined earlier as the partial forefront and primary organizational levels. Thus, given an equivalent force ratio and similar configurations of play, progress in team sports may be seen as performing the same actions faster or solving problems brought about by a higher temporal-pressure type of play; or given identical time, progress in team sports may be seen as performing more complex actions.

Players can choose to perform only what they know how to do or what they can do. But performance in team sports appears to be determined by the most appropriate choice among the various solutions at the players' disposal and by the speed of this decision-making. In this context, it seems that play action is eventually determined by a strategy that needs to be specified, if not modified, during play. While strategic aspects rely on the conception of the game, tactical aspects are fundamental to regulation during play because they are based on successive decisions taken according to the evolution of the action. When players get away from action, they can focus both on the strategic and tactical aspects of their game because they have more time at their disposal.

Consequently, efficiency during play has nothing to do with a series of dissociated behaviors. It relies on efficient-action rules and play-organization rules (Gréhaigne & Godbout, 1995) that regulate strategic and tactical choices that are neither conscious nor directly observable. However, the existence of such rules appears to be confirmed by the fact that the player can adapt to many configurations of play and eventually state the rule or rules on which a solution was based. When teachers or researchers ask students, "What strategy did you use on that point?" (French, Werner, Taylor, Hussey, & Jones, 1996, p. 446), they are in fact trying to elicit the more or less explicit formulation of such rules. Coming back to play efficiency, one might say that tactical efficiency is a generative capacity likely to produce infinite tactical behaviors in response to infinite new configurations of play.

One must, however, differentiate between the unfolding of a static phase (a set-play) or the use of tactics in an unexpected play (Bouthier, 1988). A static phase is made up of one or many schemas of play that consist of preestablished sequences of action, linked in a specific order, and set in motion at a given signal. Thus, a set play is a program of actions. Tactics, on the other hand, build up during action, altering the players' perception of information and their considered moves according to the lessons they draw from the events of the game. Tactics imply, for the player, a capacity to use both determinism and random occurrences. On an individual basis, tactics may be defined as a subject's own operating system during play, and to fulfill his or her role, the player tries to submit as little as possible to the restraints, the uncertainties, and the hazards of the game while using them as much as possible.

A program is predetermined in its operations, and in this sense, it is automatic. Tactics are predetermined in their end result but not in all their operations, even though they must have numerous automatisms at their disposal to function properly. The program is put to use when there is little choice, little chance at play, or simply when it is necessary to play faster than the opponent. Tactics and strategy can emerge only at a conscious level where one finds available choices, faces unexpected events, and has the possibility of finding solutions to these new situations.

Tactical efficiency implies the capacity for deciding and deciding fast. This capacity rests upon the ability to conceive solutions. Thus, tactical decision-making requires knowledge. When tactics are operating, cognitive processes serve to extract information from play, to draw an adequate representation of the situation, to weigh contingencies, and to elaborate action scenarios. The resulting operative knowledge of configurations of play allows players to recognize restraints, regularities, and constants, and hence to capture and question the unexpected event to transform it into information. In a sense, tactical knowledge uses certainty, stability, and constancy to recognize and solve unexpected configurations of play.

Strategy and tactics encompass a vast number of potential decisions and actions regarding offense or defense, and it is not the intent of this book to analyze them at length. While discussing the teaching and learning of team sports, some authors have come up with categories of tactical and strategic knowledge (Gréhaigne & Godbout, 1995; Mitchell, 1996; Werner, 1989) that may be of interest to readers concerned with the substance of pedagogical content knowledge in team sports. In the present work, we have elected to consider some basic principles that may help focus the students' attention while they are discussing or considering a strategy to be implemented or are reflecting on successful or unsuccessful tactical choices. Those principles may also guide a coach when preparing the team for a match, or help a teacher plan a teaching unit.

SOME PRINCIPLES UNDERLYING STRATEGY AND TACTICS

None of the principles presented in this section relates to specific maneuvers on the part of the players. In a way, one might say that they emerge from the internal logic of invasion team sports discussed earlier. Some are linked to the force ratio; others are linked to the competency network, but all serve the same general purpose—overcoming the opponents in view of victory. For the sake of clarity and generalization, the principles are examined separately and in general terms in relation to the reality of the game. Essentially, it is their combination and contextualization that generate success. At times, certain principles may apply more to strategy and others to tactics, but each of them should be seen as eventually bearing consequences for both aspects of the game.

- **The deception principle.** This principle relates to trying to deceive and trick the opponent into making a bad move or a poor response. In team sports, this principle is used at all levels, on a collective or individual basis. Everyone knows that on an individual basis, numerous players make use of fakes to outwit their direct opponent. Deception is also possible on a collective basis, however it requires a great deal of involvement among players.

The organization of the defense to force the ball carrier to an area on the playing surface where he or she will be faced with a bad angle for shooting on goal is a good example. When a team can collectively organize their defensive actions to produce this result, the defending team's goalkeeper can easily foresee the chain of events potentially leading to a shot on the goal, knowing that this shot will be coming from a bad angle.

- **The surprise principle.** This is the most-used principle when a team attacks with several interlocked sequences of play. A winger who progresses on the outskirt on the opposite side of the ball, at the opponent's back, is obviously counting on a surprise effect. This principle is closely related to the mobility and opportunity principles. Whereas the surprise principle implies using unexpected actions, the deception principle, which may seem similar, leads opponents to act wrongly or to misinterpret the configurations of play.

- **The mobility principle.** Positional attack, based on continuity of play, requires preparation before the attack can be launched. Through fast shifting and good circulation of the ball, attackers may induce, in a given area of the attack zone, a breaking-down point in the state of equilibrium between the two teams and thus facilitate a shot on goal.

- **The opportunity principle.** Taking advantage of the opponents' mistakes is such an obvious principle that it does not deserve further development. But still, one must see the mistake and seize the occasion.

- **The cohesion principle.** For a team's objective to be achieved, there is a need for coherence of action from its conception through its execution. This requires the application of the cohesion principle on the team's part. All players must play in harmony, with everyone playing his or her part. Consequently, the logical, rational aspects of thoughts and actions cannot ignore the affective counterpart of the cohesion principle, that of adhesion. Depending upon teams and pursued objectives, this enduring cohesion may bear a higher or a lesser energy cost for maintaining the group. At times, this maintenance cost may be at the expense of the productive energy required by the confrontation with the other team.

- **The competency principle.** Coherence and cohesion are obtained, in part, through the competency network that entails different roles and functions among players. This way, the whole acquires a certain homogeneity that makes it possible to lower the maintenance energy cost. Indeed, competency at all levels and at all positions brings about, in the relationships between players of a same team, a feeling of trust based on mutually recognized capacities.

- **The reserve principle.** As an example, a support organization of play is based on this principle. A support player is a player by whom the attack may be immediately restarted when a sequence of play including certain maneuvers has failed. In soccer, having the forwards carry the ball makes it possible to distribute other players and constitute a reserve along the longitudinal axis of play.

- **The economy principle.** The dynamics of reciprocal attacks, linked to scoring or to the loss of the ball, leads sometimes to a result, for example a goal, that may call for a change of objective in the case of both the winning and the losing team. For instance, simply keeping ahead in the score, instead of increasing one's advantage, brings about a change in the spirit of the play and in the attack principles. It is no longer a matter of taking initiatives in view of scoring, but rather of taking initiatives in view of keeping the ball without denying the play. This is what we call the economy principle. Whether the use of this principle is desirable in physical education classes is another matter related to the teaching-learning process per se. It should be noted that applying the economy principle forces a team, a group of players, or a specific player to think over strategic, tactical, or technical choices, as well as their cost. In this perspective, one may also think that, all things considered, it is better not to change one's game and that the cost of the successive opponents' offensive maneuvers will be enough to make their actions less and less efficient.

- **The improvement principle.** Before a match, on the basis of a subjective estimate of the force ratio, players select or elaborate consistent systems of play that they will implement with whatever tactical and technical abilities they possess at the time. At this level, technical progress is subordinated to the systems of play, in relation to the estimated force ratio and the selected strategic principles. A deeper knowledge of and a higher degree of integration to the implemented systems of play may make it easier for a player to decode opponents' and partners' play and, thus, to act faster. But this gain, obtained through automation, may be counterbalanced by the opponents' knowledge. Indeed the opponent may in turn, through a similar fast decoding of the play, offer a more attuned opposition to the player's actions. Then, a progress dynamic sets in whereby players attempt to surpass the present stage of execution to outwit the opponents.

In the present chapter, fundamental features of team sports and games, the notion of oppositional relationship, the force ratio, and the competency network have been presented. The notions of strategy and tactics have been differentiated, and various principles related to the force ratio and underlying strategy and tactics have been examined. In the next chapter, the goal will be to define and refine the notion of *configuration of play* and show how it can be used to analyze team sports.

4

DECISION-MAKING IN TEAM SPORTS

Game play intelligence is the result of a combination of flair, resource-fulness, vigilant attention, a sense of opportunity, and so on. Based on this description, emphasis is always put on "practical efficiency" to attain success during game play. A player's practical efficiency must be flexible to adapt to constant, varying game situations. Instead of developing one model that will constitute a norm for his or her game play action, a player should focus on the flow of play and the play configuration at hand to detect its coherence and to profile its evolution. One has to detect favorable factors within a given configuration of play and base oneself upon the situation's potential to try and take advantage of it.

CONFIGURATION OF PLAY

In a broad sense, a configuration is a list or a schematic providing the nature and the main characteristics of all elements of a given system. In relation to team games and sports, the notion of configuration of play refers to the relative positioning of players on both teams in relation to the possession and the location of the projectile ball, puck, and so on and in relation to the various players' movements. At times, it is also referred to as a pattern of play (Ali, 1988), a situation of play (McPherson, 1993), or a display (McMorris & Graydon, 1997). During the game, players need to study the shift from one configuration of play to another to better understand the evolution of play. In soccer, for instance, attackers who have moved the ball to the center of the field and who realize that the defenders have spread themselves across the field may elect to go on with an attack, exploiting the depth of the field to get closer to the goal. In basketball, once a team realizes that they are facing a zone defense, attackers can choose to shoot from the periphery. Another choice could be to pass the ball to a player located behind the defenders in the front of the play space, where players are effectively engaged in the action.

During the game, a configuration of play evolves from state 1 to state 2 and so on to state N as long as the ball remains in play. There are two ways of looking at this situation. First, the configuration of play may be defined by the positions of the players at a certain moment (Gréhaigne, Bouthier, & David, 1997). This would lead to a static, two-dimensional study of the spatial distribution of attackers and defenders and of the position of the ball. Considering several successive configurations of play at this point, like a series of still photographs, one could determine the reasons for attackers' and defenders' choices of action.

Another way of considering the problem in a more dynamic manner consists of defining the microstate of the attack/defense system on the basis of location, direction, and the possible speed of all players, including the ball carrier and the ball itself, involved in the confrontation system at this moment. Then, each microstate is determined by a distribution of the players and the ball on the playing surface with regard to their respective locations, orientations, and speed of displacement (Gréhaigne et al., 1997). Considering such dynamic configurations of play represents a more elaborate means for describing the reality of the game. In connection with perceptual and decision-making skills, the construct of configuration of play appears crucial because it makes it possible for the players to optimize their activity during play.

One can think that, to detect pertinent clues in a given configuration of play, a novice needs to be guided with precise landmarks. These precise and simple reference elements are probable indicators of the evolution of the game play situation, and they make it possible for the novice to ignore many parameters useless for adequately dealing with the configuration of play. Configurations of the game vary because players' actions bring in purposeful or random changes. Dealing adequately with a configuration of play means that a player makes a pertinent analysis of its characteristics and potential and makes an appropriate decision. However, there may be more than one pertinent analysis applicable to a configuration of play. As the opposition evolves, new relations are created between elements of the game and others are destroyed; thus there is always a production of endless, instantaneous states of equilibrium. From a player's point of view, all these relations that constitute the whole set of configurations are not equally interesting. Some are not at stake, and the player can ignore them; others must be recognized because they are the ones that must prompt the production of an adequate response in the shortest possible time.

Two notions are at the centre of the game analysis process:

1. **Game play configuration** as it actualizes itself and takes form in the force ratio between opposing teams
2. **The situation's potential** that a player or team has to take advantage of

Consequently, a player must base him or herself on the situation's potential to make a decision and formulate an adequate response (the notion of "cascade of decisions" from Deleplace, 1979). Hence, the idea of determining the course of game play events based on a predetermined plan is excluded. Evaluation and even prognostication are at the forefront of decision-making and replace the idea of a predetermined plan.

From a precise reference framework, the opposition relationship can be assessed to detect a situation's potential that can, in turn, be exploited. The assessment of the force ratio between opponents in the presence of a game situation's potential represents a key moment in a player's reflection. The player must consider the promising factors in the game play configuration that he or she has concluded could play favorably. Within an antagonistic process, interaction is continuous. Also, a player can perceive, at any moment, what is profitable to his or her team and reciprocally, what can be damaging to the opposing team. A situation's potential is determinant in a team's profit or loss since it is the factor that permits players to reorient a game situation. To conceive game efficiency in this manner, a player's game behaviors or responses must be considered not as an application of a preconceived plan but as an exploitation of the potential in a given game situation.

Instead of elaborating game plans that are projected for use in future game situations and defining the different means to effectively use these game plans, the teacher or coach must help players adequately assess the factors within a given game play configuration that will lead to positive game responses. These are often unforeseen, novel circumstances that require game-related wisdom for a team to effectively profit from them. A good player's tactics should consist of influencing the evolution of a game configuration by exerting pressure on the play. By doing this, the goal is to create a game configuration that will be advantageous to the offense. Once exploited, a game situation's potential should lead to a favorable configuration of play.

DECISION-MAKING IN SPORTS

Any voluntary action involves not only some level of motor skill—to ensure efficient execution—but also the choice to perform the action. In some instances, the choice may be simple, based on a yes-or-no context. In other more complex situations, there may be a need not only to decide whether to act, but also to choose among different courses of action. For instance, once one has made the decision to move a heavy object, one might pull, push, roll, or carry the object; place it in a wheelbarrow; and so on, depending upon the form of the object, the characteristics of the surroundings, one's strength, and so on. One's daily life is filled with decision-action dyads of this nature.

Among the various types of activity humans engage in, sports offer a unique context: Whether for the sake of leisure or profession, one competes against oneself or against others with the intent of winning. In individual sports, decisions will be made to ensure that one goes faster, jumps higher, throws further, and so on. Most of the time, such decisions are made well in advance. When the time comes to perform, the action is conducted accordingly. In sports where two people confront each other, the object is to "play" against somebody else and to perform better, knowing that the other is trying to do the same. Although general plans of action may have been established prior to the encounter, each player is faced with many decisions during the match as each one tries to outwit the other.

In this respect, team sports offer an even more complex situation, providing a bigger challenge in terms of decision-making. Thus for each player on both teams, playing well means choosing the right course of action at the right moment, performing that course of action efficiently, and doing this over and over throughout the match. To illustrate the complexity of team sports, Bouthier (1993) has presented a model (shown in Figure 4.1) that helps put decision-making and efficient action into perspective.

This model highlights the interdependent nature of all identified components. As one can see, the choice of pertinent solutions and decision-making are heavily related to the remaining components. During game play, the player must make decisions about actions to be undertaken. The player devises plans in accordance with strategic decisions and makes adjustments as effective action proceeds. Adjustments are based on tactical decisions (Bouthier & Savoyant, 1984; Gréhaigne & Godbout, 1995; Gréhaigne, Godbout, & Bouthier, 1999).

The two types of decisions are very much influenced by the social values of the group that the player is part of and by the player's personal

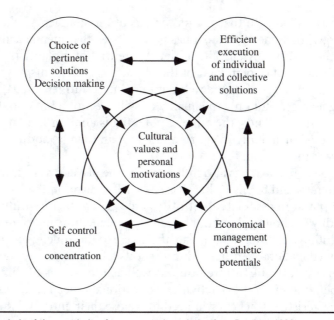

Fig. 4.1 Analysis of the complexity of team sports (translation from Bouthier, 1993).

motives regarding the activity (Nuttin, 1985; Leontiev, 1976; Bouthier, 1993; Bouthier, Pastré, & Samurçay, 1995). Cultural and motivational factors play an important role in the choice of solutions and in the degree of engagement in the action. Reciprocally, the development of decision-making competencies reinforces motivation. It is thus critical that in educational settings, students be put into situations where they can relate to real life contexts, which should help them to give significance to their learning activity.

Any decision with regard to the context and theory of play becomes valid only if it can be efficiently translated into action. This implies that the player actually has at his or her disposal a range of corresponding responses (i.e., individual and collective technical skills and tactics). However, players tend to favor, among possible answers, those valued by the group to which they belong. Reciprocally, the mastering of technical and tactical skills reinforces motivation. Thus, although tactics make up the context that justifies the use of particular technical skills, these skills should not be perceived as secondary. Technical skills constitute the tools for tactics (Mahlo, 1974). Thus, the educational setting, instead of opposing technical and tactical learning, should rather articulate them in a "tactical–technical" education.

It is well known that the motor execution of a tactical choice costs energy. For some 10 years, it has been noticed that mental activity consumes energy as well. The athletic potential of a player is therefore important not only in view of the physical requirements of game play, but also in view of its mental requirements(Bouthier, 1989a). Indeed, fatigue affects not only the quality of skill execution but also the lucidity of choices. Thus, the athletic potential is another limitation factor for decision-making in sport, and its use in turn is modulated by the player's motivation.

Decision-making is also influenced by the player's concentration and awareness and by his or her degree of self-control in the face of stress and pleasure associated with the game. These factors influence the lucidity of choices, though they can at the same time interfere with skill execution and limit or stimulate the access to the athletic potential.

In educational settings, critical aspects and moments of the game to focus on must be pointed out, as well as modalities of self-control. Depending upon sport activities, educational objectives and students' characteristics, teachers will need to choose their entry point and their intervention levers among the various components of sport action presented in the model.

RESEARCH ON DECISION-MAKING AND SPORTS

Most of the research on decision-making in sports appears to have been conducted in connection with expertise (McMorris & Graydon, 1997; Ripoll, 1991; Tennenbaum, 1999). As will be discussed later, it is not our intent to strictly apply all the conclusions reached in this type of research. However, it is of interest to note that some constructs considered in research on expertise in sport should be considered when teaching decision-making in physical education or recreational and competitive sport. In the context of this book, we will refer to children and adolescent learners involved in these types of programs as *novices*.

Although research results are not unequivocal as to differences between experts and novices (McMorris & Graydon, 1997), it is generally agreed that experts make faster and more accurate decisions when predicting an opponent's response (Chamberlain & Coelho, 1993; McPherson, 1993; Williams & Grant, 1999). Thus, they display greater anticipation skills. Chamberlain and Coelho (1993) recognized that experts make more accurate decisions based on earlier-occurring information. At the same time these authors stated that, in general, experts tend to have an advantage in the speed of decisions made, but not necessarily in the accuracy of their decisions. However, this advantage is context specific, meaning it is related to the expert's area of expertise.

> The superior decision-making capabilities of the experts appears to be due not only to a more extensive declarative knowledge structure (factual knowledge, consisting of if–then statements) but to a well developed procedural knowledge base (actions plans, the "do" statements). The disadvantage for the novice, then, is the lack of context-specific declarative and procedural knowledge base leads to a more generalized approach to problem solving, resulting in slower access to information needed for arriving at accurate decisions (Chamberlain & Coelho, 1993, p. 148).

There appears to be agreement in the literature with reference to experts' superior knowledge base both declarative and procedural, as opposed to experts' superior visual characteristics or aptitudes (e.g., French & McPherson, 1999; McPherson, 1993; McPherson, 1999; Nevett & French, 1997; Williams, Davids, Burwitz, & Williams, 1993; Williams & Grant, 1999). As pointed out by French and McPherson (1999), experts also display better problem representation in the sense that they are better at accessing the right portion of their knowledge base to perform specific sport tasks.

Thus, research findings acknowledge that anticipation, prediction, and decision-making are key elements for performance in sports. In both cases, speed is critical (Steinberg, Chaffin, & Singer, 1998), whereas accuracy is a necessary but insufficient condition.

It has also been recommended that perception and action be coupled for the analysis of experts' performance (Bouthier, 1989b; Chamberlain & Coelho, 1993; Williams et al., 1993; Williams & Grant, 1999). This suggests that when considering the development of decision-making skills, anticipation, decision-making, and effective action should be associated whenever reflection on action is sought.

Selective attention (McMorris & Beazeley, 1997; Ripoll & Benguigui, 1999) and attention orienting (Nougier & Rossi, 1999) have been evoked in connection with decision-making and should therefore be considered in learning activities in light of students' concentration capabilities. As suggested by Magill (1998), attention can then be oriented toward information-rich aspects of the game as opposed to specific cues. This is very much in line with a constructivist view of the teaching-learning process.

Deliberate systematic and long-term practice is considered essential for the acquisition of expert performance skills (Ericsson & Charness, 1994; Ericsson, Krampe, & Tesch-Römer, 1993). Many authors acknowledge that it may take as many as 10 years of practice to develop expertise (Ericsson & Simon, 1993; French & McPherson, 1999; Helsen, Starkes, & Hodges, 1998; Thomas & Thomas, 1999). In connection with deliberate practice, simulation techniques have been tried (Williams & Grant, 1999) as well as other learning activities more closely related to the actual practice of sport (Helsen et al., 1998).

Given the objectives pursued by school physical education programs and the time constraints imposed on regular physical education programs, many research findings on deliberate practice may appear irrelevant for the teaching of decision-making in sport. However, one can at least assume that if a minimal level of performance is to be achieved, some form of deliberate practice ought to be put in place, as opposed to play sessions (McMorris, 1999) and should display ecological validity, that is, guided direct practice and experience with the task should be allowed (Williams et al., 1993).

Finally, verbal reports are seen as an important strategy to obtain information on the thought processes of experts and novices (French & McPherson, 1999; McPherson, 1993). We view overt verbalization as a means to focus one's, overt verbalization will be discussed not as a measurement strategy per se, but as a mean to focus one's attention on one's thought process, to exchange information with one's partners, and to stimulate critical thinking.

ELEMENTS INVOLVED IN DECISION-MAKING

Faced with some event, one interprets reality and gives it meaning. In team sports, what is happening during a sequence of play actions? What interacting elements can one identify? Discussing the complexity of decision-making in team games, McMorris and Graydon (1997) write:

> Knowing which cues to process, however, does not guarantee successful decision making. The cues must be perceived accurately. The inter-relationship between attackers and defenders and, in particular, the space behind, between and in front of them, must be determined. This information will tell players what options are open to them in that particular situation. This

can be compared with past experience of similar situations and, based on that comparison, a decision of what action to take can be made. In making a decision, however, the players should, also, take into account their own abilities, the abilities of the opposition, the physical conditions in which the game is being played, the score at that particular moment and the area of the field in which the action is taking place (McMorris & MacGillivary, 1988) Furthermore, the situation is exacerbated by the fact that players often have to make decisions quickly, if the initiative is not to be lost (p. 71).

In Figure 4.2, a selected number of elements that are likely to influence each player's successive decisions during sequences of action are identified. As illustrated in this model, decision-making may be seen as triggered by a play action that offers a given configuration of play. As discussed earlier, this configuration of play will likely be perceived and interpreted differently by the various players involved in the action, and by outside observers as well, and may thus lead to differentiated decision-making. Both perception, related more or less to selective attention, and subsequent decision-making may be influenced by a series of elements. Some of these elements, listed on the right side of the figure, depend upon each player considered individually. Others, listed on the left side of the Figure 4.2, reflect the collective aspect of the game, which each player must also take into account.

Fig. 4.2 Some elements of the decision-making process in team sports (translation from Gréhaigne & Godbout, 1999a).

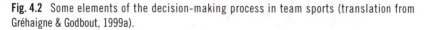

INDIVIDUAL ASPECTS OF DECISION-MAKING

While team sports imply the presence of teammates, choices of action rest ultimately upon each player. Decision-making elements related to each individual player are as follows:

- **Individual strategy.** Individual strategy is a type of advanced planning based on one's hypotheses of likely actions undertaken by one's opponents and partners (Gréhaigne, Godbout, & Bouthier, 1999); this prior planning may well influence the player's selective attention, and it gives a particular orientation to decisions that will be taken during the game before play has even started.
- **Player's cognitive map or knowledge base.** The declarative and procedural knowledge accumulated through past experience influences the player's interpretation of a configuration of play perceived in connection with efficient action rules (Gréhaigne & Godbout, 1995).
- **Tactical knowledge.** This type of knowledge may rest on some theoretical concepts but remains mostly experiential, based on notions extracted from practice. Once the configuration of play has been perceived, the player may make sense of it or not. The recall of successful or unsuccessful solutions helps players assess the relevance of such responses. Thus, strategic and tactical knowledge orients decision-making. The recall may rest on long term memory, involving some action plan profile, and on short term memory, focusing on events related to the unfolding game at hand and involving some current event profile.
- **Players' resources.** Knowledge about and consciousness of one's present resources serve as a filter, allowing the player to consider or reject certain action hypotheses offhand. Such resources may concern the player's level and range of general motor skills, motor competencies, and sport specific motor skills. In many cases, especially in invasion type team sports where attackers must invade the defenders' camp to score and thus cover much more ground, such resources will also concern the player's physiological response capacity, considering the energy cost of hypothesized courses of action. Although not necessarily at a conscious level, other variable characteristics of the player, such as concentration level and motivation, may also enhance or hinder perception and decision-making.
- **Player's location and posture.** A player's location and posture determine the possibilities of the player's responses given his or

her resources; a wrong perception of one's position and posture may negatively affect decision-making.

COLLECTIVE ASPECTS OF DECISION-MAKING

Collective aspects of the game may also influence each player's perception and decision-making. Gréhaigne et al. (1999) present three aspects that must be considered in efficient collective decision-making.

- **The collective strategy.** The collective strategy refers to the various plans, principles, or action guidelines selected prior to the match in view of organizing the activity of the players and the team as a whole during the competition. The strategy put together may either concern major general play options, or specify the players' behavior for various categories of play situations. Thus, collective strategy may direct, in advance, a given player's attention toward specific aspects of the game and orient the general trend of one's decision-making process.
- **The force ratio.** The force ratio refers to the antagonistic links that exist between several players or between the two groups of players brought together in an opposition relationship by virtue of certain rules of the game that determine an interaction mode. Advanced hypotheses about the force ratio and the actual perception during the encounter may well orient, in part, the player's individual strategy and tactical adaptation throughout the match.
- **The competency network.** The competency network is made up of the various relations between the players within a team. As discussed by Gréhaigne et al. (1999), it influences the players' play actions and behaviors depending upon their status within the team and the force ratio encountered. In a sense, the competency network may not directly influence a player's decision-making, but its weight is implicit since it is taken into account in the collective if not the individual strategy. Thus, the competency network will normally orient the attribution of specific roles to each player; hence its influence on decision-making.

Although considered separately for the sake of the discussion, the various individual and collective elements presented above are somewhat interwoven. For instance, the blending of each player's cognitive map, tactical knowledge, and resources leads to the recognition of a given competency network, and both the force ratio and the competency network orient the planning of collective and individual strategies. More stable elements, such as the competency network, the force ratio, the cognitive map, part of the tactical knowledge or action plan profile, and part of the player's resources (e.g., motor skills), constitute a meshed background that filters the perception–interpretation–anticipation–decision sequence. As the play action unfolds, more changing elements such as the player's location and posture, the level of one's fatigue and motivation, and the current event profile add their weight and ultimately determine a more or less stable chain of relevant and irrelevant decisions.

The whole set of elements can come into play only at a superior cognitive level where one can make choices, face unexpected events, and find solutions for new situations. At this point, cognitive processes serve to extract information from play, to make up an adequate representation of the situation, to assess potential events, and to draw up action scenarios.

There appear to be two theories at hand. According to supporters of one theory (Bayer, 1979; Famose, 1996; Parlebas, 1976), the larger a player's knowledge base, the more this player can recognize constraints, regularities, and constants, and the more the player can take notice of and question unexpected, unforeseen events. Knowledge, from a decision-making point of view, must rely on both certainty and fixed and stable references to confront and solve uncertainty. Thus, at the level of perceptual and decision-making mechanisms, learning consists of an increase in the amount of memorized knowledge and an improvement in the process of structuring perceptual knowledge into procedural knowledge (Famose, 1996).

Concerning the management and the organization of play, supporters of a second theory (Deleplace, 1979; Gréhaigne, 1989) contend that an expert can clearly seize a larger amount of information useful for the solving of problems brought about by the game compared to novices. Nevertheless, this amount of information remains relatively limited, and it is the quality of the information that is determining. In that respect, prior analysis of the internal logic of the sport by a coach, a teacher, or some other expert provides useful data. Based on such analyses, one can draw the player's attention to typical patterns of play. This way the player has at his or her disposal an already-worked-out mental action picture instead of being burdened by a mass of information not useful for the solving of the problem at hand.

The problem for a player is to succeed in encompassing the entire complexity of the game within a system made of the smallest possible number of fundamental action axes interrelated in a strong logical and functional unit. Tactics are based on successive decisions, taken according to the evolution of the action. The development of tactical capacity implies the development of a capacity for quick decisions. In turn, this capacity relies on one's capacity for conceiving solutions. In a word, the development of a capacity for choosing requires the development of knowledge and routines. Consequently, the player, through cumulative experience, builds up an actual action matrix by always assimilating and refining the data collected into a personal mental action picture that allows him or her to act and react faster.

One can use an operative model of decision-making that emphasizes the contributions of some of the elements discussed earlier. Such a dynamic model reflects the reality of a game played under strong time constraints. One hypothesis is to consider that the player's analysis of play action under strong time constraints is conducted with reference to a few typical configurations of play and to related forerunner cues that allow a player to anticipate upcoming play. Knowing the essentials of appropriate responses to given configurations of play facilitates fast decision-making (Bouthier, David, & Eloi, 1994).

This chapter exposed how an accurate analysis of the configurations of game play allows a player to identify components of decision-making. In chapter 5, a few ideas on the notion of *tactical knowledge in team sports* will be presented.

5

THE PLAYER'S TACTICAL KNOWLEDGE

In a study on the formative evaluation practices of physical education teachers, Gréhaigne, Billard, Guillon, and Roche (1988) registered and analyzed the didactic communications of teachers during sequences of play. They noted that these communications contained orders and rules given from the edge of the playing surface during game situations. However, in the teachers' comments at the end of the sequence, nothing was said in connection with such rules or advice. Gréhaigne and his colleagues believe that rules and advice constituted declarative knowledge about the game at hand but that such knowledge had to be more systematically and formally identified (Marsenach & Mérand, 1987).

In this chapter we will concentrate on the fundamental components which constitute tactical knowledge as this knowledge is critical to overall game performance.

THE CONTENT OF TACTICAL KNOWLEDGE IN INVASION TEAM SPORTS AND GAMES

To identify tactical knowledge, Gréhaigne (1996) systematically collected action rules that were stated during game situations either by the students or by the teachers. Then, through content analysis, categories of rules were progressively identified. The categories were regularly validated in two ways: The categories were submitted twice to groups of experts on team sport and to a group of physical educators. They tested this tactical knowledge while teaching team sports to secondary school students and submitted suggestions and corrections based upon the relevance or the lack of relevance of various action rules (Gréhaigne & Laroche, 1994).

From our perspective, tactical knowledge is fundamentally "knowledge in action" because for a player, tactical awareness and performance are strongly linked. According to Gréhaigne (1992) and Malglaive (1990), knowledge in team sports rests upon action rules, play organization rules, and motor capacities. Action rules define conditions to be enforced and elements to be taken into account if one wants to ensure efficient action (Goirand, 1993; Gréhaigne, 1989; Gréhaigne & Guillon, 1991; Marin, 1993; Vergnaud, Halbvacks, & Rouchier, 1978). Such rules, which are basic to tactical knowledge about the game, and their use, whether isolated or in connection with other rules, provide an answer to a given problem. They represent a momentary truth, and some rules can become obstacles to progress on other occasions. For instance, to *create open space, one must tighten up the defense in one zone and swiftly pass the ball to another zone.*

Table 5.1 and Table 5.2 present a nonexhaustive list of action rules and related principles of actions for the attack and the defense. Action rules constitute an interesting notion in relation to learning and can be used as a theoretical tool for elaborating curricula in relation to the teaching-learning process of team sports.

ACTION RULES

Vergnaud, Halbvachs, & Rouchier (1978) define action rules as rules that permit a player to generate actions based on certain situational variables. These variables can evolve through time, from one situation to another. One rule, or a set of rules, however, can be applied to or associated with a class of game play problems. Gréhaigne et al. (1988) state that action rules define the conditions to be respected and the elements that need to be considered to produce efficient action. For example, when trying to free oneself from a marker, a player must be available and accessible to the ball carrier. The rules can be characterized in the following manner: They are conscious, they contribute to comprehension and selection in relation to motor competencies, and they contribute to the execution of action. Action rules also contribute to the explanation of action.

From a functional point of view, action rules constitute one of the principal sources of tactical knowledge. They permit teammates to exchange ideas among themselves or with the teacher or coach. From this perspective, action rules serve as irreplaceable support for communication. They lead players to verbalization and game play awareness and, hence, increase the players' precision in the analysis of a game situation.

TABLE 5.1 Offensive Action Rules and Related Principles of Action

Keeping the ball[4]

Having at one's disposal a maximum number of potentials receivers or increasing the possibilities of exchange

Protecting the ball (using one's body as an obstacle)

Keeping the ball away from the opponent and close to oneself

Directing passes into space behind the defender and in front of the attacker

Moving to be at passing distance, seen by the ball-owner, away from the defender

Playing in movement

Reducing the number of exchanges required to reach the scoring zone

Reducing the time used to bring the ball into the scoring zone and shoot

Varying the rhythm and the intensity of the moves

Moving when space is free

Creating passing angles

Passing the ball ahead of the receiver

Favoring instantaneous passes

Continuing movement after having released the ball

Receiving the ball while moving

Exploiting and creating available space

Using the depth and the width of the field or court

Locking the defense in one zone and playing in another

Alternating direct play, indirect play, short passes, and long passes

Locking opponents to free some partners

Changing the direction of play

Using spaces not occupied by opponents

Moving away from opponents, into the intervals or to the back of the opponents

Creating screens or blocks and exploiting them

Using speed and temporal advantages

Creating uncertainty

Keeping the alternative direct play/indirect play

Changing one's rhythm (slow/quick)

Luring opponents into one zone to conclude in another

Increasing the number of players involved in the action

Faking or combining the change of rhythm, space, and orientation

Moving in one direction and releasing the ball in another

Adopting a posture or an orientation that allows various actions (i.e., disguising one's intentions)

Adapted and reprinted, by permission, from Gréhaigne & Godbout, 1995, pp. 490–505.

TABLE 5.2 Defensive Action Rules and Related Principles of Action

Defending the target

Initiate pressure in the area of the ball in the few seconds following a loss of possession
Putting as many players as possible between the ball and the target
Reinforcing and covering constantly the axis of the goal
Organizing the team along lines of strength
Putting the attack off center, towards the outskirts
Moving the ball away
Covering one's partners
Preventing shots
Withdrawing quickly while looking at the ball to recreate the defensive lines

Regaining possession of the ball

Recovering the ball as close as possible to the opponents' goal
Increasing the numerical density in the middle of the field and in the attack area
Impairing the progression of the ball
Challenging every opponent
Looking for the interception
Putting immediate pressure on the player with the ball—harassment
Positioning oneself on likely ball trajectories to isolate the ball carrier from his or her teammates

Challenging the opponents' progression

Reducing uncertainty
Reducing the number of potential receivers
Foreseeing opponents' actions
Understanding quickly the opponents' system of play to stabilize the perception
Having an explicit communication within the defense. (A player must coordinate the defense)
Evaluating the capacity and skills of one's direct opponent
Keeping both the attackers and the ball in view
Sticking to agreed rules and to one's task
Impairing the opponent through one's placement and movements
Faking to trick one's opponent
Reducing the time, space, and options
Modifying rapidly one's defensive system to adapt it to the game
Adopting an optimal position on the field
Reducing available space
Keeping the attack away from the target
Defining everybody's rules on set plays
Spotting the favorite sector of one's direct opponent's actions
Reducing the effective space available to one's opponent
Delaying the attack whenever the defenders are outnumbered

Reprinted, by permission, from Gréhaigne & Godbout, 1995, pp. 490–505.

Action rules can be contradictory and even opposite depending on the oppositional relationship within a particular configuration of play. For example, when a team is faced with a situation where it needs to maximize the number of available and accessible players for potential ball exchanges and to cover adequately the axis of their own goal, the specific action rules that a team has to respect differ greatly. Practically speaking, when facing certain problematic configurations of play, the confrontations, which require contradictory action rules, force players to reason in a dialectic way. Players must be able to interpret action rules, test them, and if needed, infringe on or redefine them. In a sense, a player must rely on theoretical knowledge in relation to action rules but not be dependant on it. Thus, a player must be critical, pragmatic, and opportunistic to profit from a configuration of play. Hence, through inference, we find that decisions made during game play leave a mental trace due to their use, evolution and their evaluation. This type of analysis is not always easy because action rules that are well integrated become, over time, *habitus* (Bourdieu, 1972, 1980; Gréhaigne, Richard, Mahut, & Griffin, 2002). Bourdieu (1972) defines *habitus* as:

> A system of durable, transposable arrangements that, while integrating past experiences, functions like a perception matrix that can make the accomplishment of different tasks possible thanks to the analogical transfer of schemas that permits one to resolve problems of the same nature. (pp. 178–179)

Based on this definition, *habitus* is simply a player's singular experience and constitutes a nonconscious mode of functioning during game play.

Finally, action rules that are associated with a class of game play problems can be centered on a principle of efficient action, for example "playing in movement" when trying to move the ball into the offensive zone and effectively score.

THE EMERGENCE OF ACTION RULES

To achieve success during game play, the learner gathers information during action and then tries to apply it when facing different play sequences. Through experimentation, he or she can define tactical and technical responses to be used in different situations. After using these responses, the learner can then verify the gap between the expected outcomes of these responses and what actually happens. The learner can then redefine his or her action plan, if necessary, or find other alternatives for efficient action. For example, if players notice that from their 16 ball possessions, their team recovered 5 balls close to the opposition's goal, which resulted in 3 of their 4 goals, then this team should realize that ball recovery closer to the opposition's goal must be emphasized to maximize offensive potential. When these efficient action means are used successively over time and become constant, they basically become action rules. When defined, action rules become a reference framework from which a player can "actively regulate" (Piaget, 1974) him or herself to produce more efficient motor responses. However, it must be noted that the emergence of action rules does not necessarily mean a transformation in motor responses. A particular motor response can be defined as being the sum of, or the juxtaposition of, action rules. A motor response is always original and often complex and represents a player's organization when facing a particular game situation.

THE USE OF ACTION RULES

To better position game play problems in context, we will group together knowledge about game play and knowledge within game play in one category, which we will call "knowledge in action." This new category of knowledge emphasizes our concern in relation to the development of a player's game knowledge and skills, both tactical and technical, to be more efficient during game play. In regard to action rules, their use in an isolated situation or in combination with other rules (i.e., play organization rules) constitutes a response to a particular problem. Action rules represent a momentary truth, which can be inoperative at times and can even be an obstacle to a team's progress in other instances.

During game play, the notion of action is not only associated with the player's execution of action but also with a player's exploration of game-related knowledge through reflection on different game situations. Through this mental process, a player can analyze compatible and contradictory responses to different game situations. The goal of this experimental process, which requires effort from the player, is for the player to find coherent and economical ways of responding to game play constraints.

During the development of such knowledge, novices employ general and isolated responses, whereby the conditions in which the action is unfolding are examined partially, successively, and in a hierarchical way. Their game knowledge having evolved, intermediate players' responses are more refined, sophisticated, and discriminative; hence, they have a more tactical connotation. Intermediate players are more aware of the possible confrontational conditions between two teams. They consider explicit and implicit characteristics of play configurations that are often brought back to a few simple characteristics of game play.

It seems that learning action rules during a player's developmental phase is extremely important. During this phase, game situations are often modified (i.e., time constraints, smaller playing surface, smaller equipment, etc.), which can help players, through action rules, develop an action plan in advance based on the game situation's various elements. For example, in a 3 vs. 3 modified practice situation, where the emphasis is for a team to keep possession of the ball for three successive passes to score a point, the offensive team will apply previously learned action rules to develop efficient action within the parameters presented by this situation. Though this game situation is based on previously learned action rules, new action rules can also be learned. In a learning situation of this type, a player's cognitive activity is different from a real match situation because it permits the learner to develop awareness through experimentation and verbalization without hampering actual performance.

Play organization rules cover a certain number of themes related to the logic of the activity, the dimensions of the play area, the distribution of players on the field, and a differentiation of roles. These rules also cover a few simple organizational principles that may facilitate the elaboration of a strategy. For instance, due to the shape of the target, defenders in soccer and hockey must constantly maintain a defensive configuration protecting the central axis to throw the attackers off center. Table 5.3 presents a series of examples of such organization rules.

MOTOR CAPACITIES

Motor capacities refer to two large categories of problems related to the perceptual and decision-making activity of the player in close connection with the motor competencies that he or she possesses or must develop. Indeed, if they are to be applied, action rules require the development of motor capacities; thus rules and motor capacities can hardly be disassociated. A player's motor competencies are his or her resources from a skill execution point of view. The motor competencies that a player has at his or her disposition have a major influence on a player's repertoire of possible game play decisions. The speed of play will also greatly influence a player's decisions, even if he or she does possess a wide repertoire of motor competencies. For instance, for the ball carrier to effectively deal with a ball request from a teammate, the open player must be available and accessible.

TABLE 5.3 Play Organization Rules

Prior to the Game

Adopting a given plan of defense
Adopting a given system of play, a general framework
Assigning an optimal position on the field (or on the court) for each player
Identifying one's strength and weaknesses and those of the team
Constructing a game plan
Assigning roles and tasks within the team

During the Game

Creating imbalance in one's favor
Coordinating and connecting the various actions of the team
Playing into weak axis of the opponent's defense
Maintaining movement in the game
Gaining and keeping an advance on defensive replacement
Positioning everyone optimally along the axis and at the outskirts of the field or
  the court
Leaving the ball to the opponents and choosing the right moment to regain
  possession
Adapting rapidly to the specific details of the opponent's attack and defense

Reprinted, by permission, from Gréhaigne & Godbout, 1995, pp. 490–505.

PRINCIPLES OF ACTION

Based on a number of related action rules, efficient principles of action—each defined as a theoretical structure and an operative instrument—orient various actions, making it possible to act on reality (Gréhaigne et al., 1988). Principles of action constitute a kind of macroscopic frame of reference that makes it possible for the teacher and eventually for the student to isolate and classify noted facts. An example of this would be to observe the different elements that are necessary to move the ball effectively into the offensive zone to bring the ball in the scoring area and score.

To improve tactical knowledge players must establish guidelines on which they can base their decisions. The rules presented earlier (in Tables 5.1, 5.2, and 5.3) conceptualize goals and objectives for attacking and defending that can aid players in developing their cognitive processes, which, in turn, will be beneficial to player's' development of action rules, motor competencies, and the play organization rules needed for efficient game play responses. As stated by Giordan and De Vecchi (1987), knowing beforehand is being capable of using what we have learned to resolve a problem or clarify a situation.

In this chapter, the notion of tactical knowledge has been analyzed. From our standpoint, tactical knowledge is fundamentally "knowledge in action" because, for a player, tactical awareness and performance are strongly linked. Three general categories of knowledge that have been examined are action rules that lead to principles of action, play organization rules, and motor capacities.

In the next three chapters, different strategies will be presented to better analyze the state of game play performance. More specifically, different assessment strategies will be discussed to help players and students better understand their play in the perspective of improving performance.

6

THE ANALYSIS OF PLAY IN TEAM SPORTS

Observing game play is a key element of team sport "didactics." Due to the complexity of the environment, the temporal and spatial characteristics of players' locations and movements, as well as those of the ball, game play must be analyzed in a systematic way if one wishes to obtain dependable, reliable, and useful information. This type of analysis takes into account fixed elements such as the playing surface, but also considers other variables that are controlled by players, such as the ball, play organization rules, tactics, and so on (Gréhaigne & Godbout, 1995). The meaning of players perceptions is directly linked to the force ratio.

In addressing force ratio among players, the concept of "perceived configuration of play" is an interesting one because it makes it possible to optimize the player's activity in confrontational situations. A beginner needs a precise and advanced frame of reference to pick up relevant clues within the configuration of play. This picture or mental schema, which is a functional reflection of game play, is put together by and for the player's activity. It is by definition variable and short lived since the player's actions constantly bring about purposeful modifications.

From the standpoint of the player's activity, all relations that make up the whole perceived configuration of play are not equally interesting for analysis. Some are not relevant, and the player ignores them. Others must be acknowledged, for they are the ones that orient the production of an appropriate response within a limited time span. Often, several responses will allow the completion of the task by solving the problem at hand, but the most appropriate and most dependable response will frequently be the simplest because it is the most economical from a mechanical, energetic, emotional, and informational standpoint. A good solution implies picking up a few characteristics of the configuration, and a partial arrangement of elements that will include only the ones that are essential. By giving *a priori* precedence to certain elements of game play, the player processes these data more rapidly whenever they appear in configurations of play. At the same time the player has a limited frame of reference (i.e., in the game moment) from which to collect and interpret information.

To this end, we will describe in this chapter a few observational approaches that make it possible to analyze game play from a holistic perspective because knowing what players can and cannot do is indispensable to teaching and coaching.

OBSERVATIONAL APPROACHES IN THE ANALYSIS OF GAME PLAY

For the sake of illustration in this chapter, the approaches presented will be used in reference to soccer, but they could as well be used for European handball, basketball, field hockey, and other invasion sports.

Static Approach to Observation of Game Play

The simplest observational approach that can be used consists of considering, on one hand, the defensive zone and, on the other hand, the offensive zone. If one divides each zone, one obtains four observation areas: (a) defensive, (b) pre defensive, (c) pre offensive, and (d) offensive, as illustrated in Figure 6.1.

One could also consider the central corridors of the pitch and the two bordering corridors, as presented in Figure 6.2. This would make it possible to note play actions conducted in the "attacked goal–defended goal" axis and others carried in the peripheral corridors.

A third type of grid might consider the direct play-space with a vertical target as in soccer or handball (Figure 6.3). Due to the verticality of the target, the apparent target area varies according to the shooting angle. If one combines all previous grids, one obtains the observational grid presented in Figure 6.3.

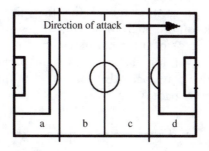

Fig. 6.1 Four observation areas.

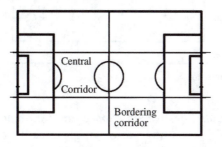

Fig. 6.2 Central and bordering corridors.

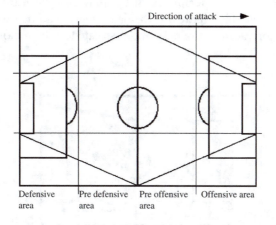

Fig. 6.3 Static observational grid.

An important feature of these tools is that they give some idea on the players' placement on the pitch, which illustrates different configurations of play. This type of information can be very useful to coaches and players in the evolution of a team's play and performance. Now we discuss the effective play-space (EP-S), the main dimensions of play, and the covered play-space (CP-S).

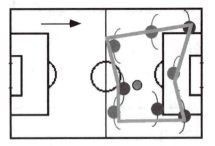

Fig. 6.4 Effective play-space.

Location of the Ball, Effective Play-Space, and Dominant Distribution If one considers a given configuration of play like the one illustrated in Figure 6.4 and Figure 6.5, one can summarize it using the notion of effective play-space (Mérand, 1977; Gréhaigne, 1989; Gréhaigne, Billard, & Laroche, 1999). The effective play-space (EP-S) may be defined as the polygonal area that one obtains by drawing a line linking all involved players located at the periphery of the play at a given instant. In the example illustrated in Figure 6.4, the ball is located at the rear of EP-S, in the central corridor (Figure 6.2), and is situated in the pre offensive area (Figure 6.1).

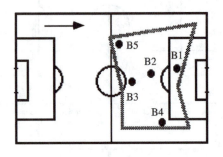

Fig. 6.5 EP-S and the location of the ball.

Due to the fact that the ball can be in different positions in relation to the effective play-space, we shall assign it to one of five categories. By convention:

1. B1 is a ball located in a central position, which is in the corridor defined by the "attacked goal/defended goal" axis, ahead of the effective play-space represented by the principal axis.
2. B2 is a ball located in a central position, in the middle of the effective play-space.
3. B3 is a ball located in a central position, at the rear of the effective play-space.
4. B4 is a ball located in a flank position either on the left or right periphery of the pitch, ahead of the effective play-space.
5. B5 is a ball located in a flank position either on the left or right periphery of the pitch, at the rear of the effective play-space.

At school, in relation to soccer in a physical education or competitive sports setting, the regular and specific player distribution on the pitch, which we call dominant distribution, presents certain constants, shown in Figure 6.6.

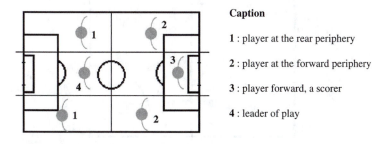

Caption

1 : player at the rear periphery

2 : player at the forward periphery

3 : player forward, a scorer

4 : leader of play

Fig. 6.6 Dominant distribution of the players.

One can use the dominant distribution to assess how players interpret the force ratio and position themselves, based on their resources, when confronting another team. Most of the time, the best players perform in the central corridor (i.e., lane), which is in the "attacked goal/defended goal" axis. More specifically, in *space-limited games*, better known as small-sided games, the best player usually stands at the rear of the effective play-space and assumes the role of the leader. The second best player is most often located at the front of the effective play-space and is given the role of scorer. The other players perform at the periphery, at the front or rear of the play-space. One can differentiate among them by noting that the more skillful player is at the forward periphery.

Indeed, players are often faced with more complex tasks, especially with regard to action on-the-ball within limited space and time. In contrast, the role of those who play at the rear periphery consists most often in clearing the ball away to keep it far from the scoring zone. Of course, one must conceive of this set of intentions and roles in a dynamic fashion. Players move around on the pitch and are led to deviate from their typical line of conduct, but generally speaking, they abide by this distribution.

Dynamic Approach to the Observation of Game Play

Movement of the Ball and Force Ratios The two analytical tools presented in this section are based on the different locations of the ball in relation to the effective play-space at the origin of the ball movement. In the rear-ball play (shown in Figure 6.7), the origin of ball movement is always at the rear with respect to the future receiver of the ball. Play usually starts with the recovery of the ball and continues until its loss to the opposition for whatever reason. In the forward-ball play, at some point during the movement of the ball, it travels backward towards a supporting player.

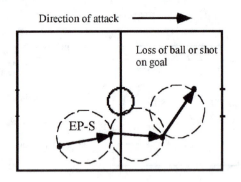

Fig. 6.7 The rear-ball play.

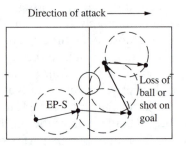

Fig. 6.8 The forward-ball play.

The transformation of the movement of the ball is the consequence of a defensive organization that creates a great difficulty for the offensive team to move the ball forward. With respect to the effective play-space, one can see a diversification of the movement of the ball (Figure 6.9).

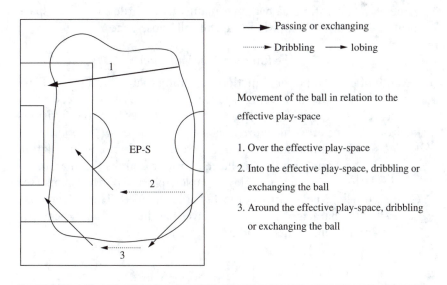

→ Passing or exchanging

┈┈► Dribbling → lobing

Movement of the ball in relation to the effective play-space

1. Over the effective play-space
2. Into the effective play-space, dribbling or exchanging the ball
3. Around the effective play-space, dribbling or exchanging the ball

Fig. 6.9 Movement of the ball regarding effective play-space.

Covered Play-Space The covered play-space (CP-S) is the area representing the space occupied by attackers and defenders during an attack. It defines the maximum space used by players throughout a sequence of play, with a succession of distortions that eventually shows the way this space has been traveled through (Figure 6.10).

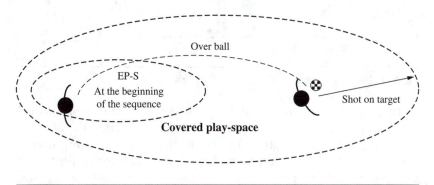

Fig. 6.10 Example of covered play-space.

SIGNIFICANT POSTURES AND BEHAVIORS

In this section, a player's level of play will be analyzed by examining his/her the postures and how he/she manipulates the ball. In this case the range of manipulation is often used as an indicator of the level of game play. For instance, a beginner mainly uses a little part of the space located in front of them, which we will call "close-space."

The Range of Manipulation

Because of gravity, players function according to a vertical plane. Players use perception to structure space on the basis of posture, or they structure it on the basis of their location with respect to a fictitious horizontal plane crossing at eye level.

The small cylinder illustrated in Figure 6.11 defines a manipulation range close to one's body. The large cylinder defines the maximum manipulation range when a player outstretches his or her arms (see Cam, Crunelle, Giana, Grosgeorge, & Labiche, 1979). These data make it possible to characterize the way a player handles the ball. A beginner uses essentially quadrants 1 and 2.

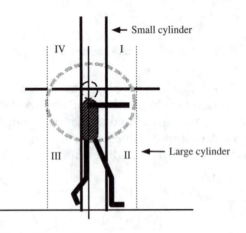

Fig. 6.11 Manipulation range in relation to the upper body.

In games where players mainly use their feet, as in soccer, a player's immediate space is constructed by increasing the manipulation range following the steps illustrated in Figure 6.12. From a manipulation restricted to the space in front of both feet, the player is able to gain possession of the ball in all positions, even with the ball coming from all directions.

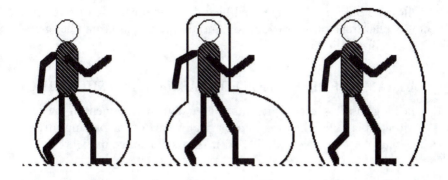

Fig. 6.12 The immediate space in soccer.

With respect to game play situations, the notion of immediate space can be specified further with the use of the following parameters: (a) the intimate-space that represents a space volume very close to the player (like a bubble); (b) the immediate-space that refers to the range of manipulation; (c) the safety distance that represents the space needed by the player to act without restraints; and finally, (d) the confrontational distance that is determined by the distance of opponents (Figure 6.13). Criteria such as the ones discussed in the

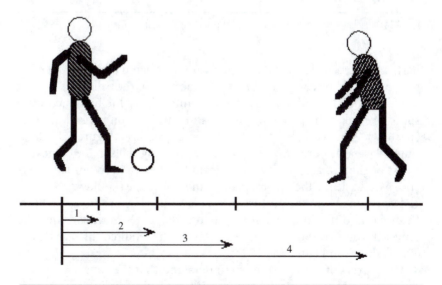

Fig. 6.13 1: Intimate space; 2: Immediate space; 3: Safety distance; 4: Confrontation distance.

following paragraph offer a viable and pertinent frame of reference for explaining a player's evolution and the way a player handles game play confrontations.

A FRAME OF REFERENCE FOR PASSING AND SHOOTING

The long pass in soccer represents one fundamental element in the evolution of play, allowing one to use a major part of the playing surface for long play (Amicale ENSEP, 1977). This is illustrated in Figure 6.14.

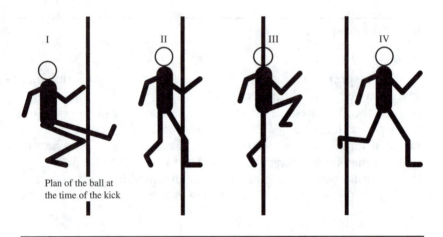

Fig. 6.14 Players' typical postures for a pass or a shot on a goal in soccer.

Part I of Figure 6.14 shows a beginner who stays behind the plane defined by the vertical line corresponding to the location of the ball at the time of the kick. A higher skilled player who wants to give the ball maximum speed overtakes the plane of the ball and falls back on his kicking foot (part IV). This requires both strength and precision. Figure 6.15 illustrates players' postures according to their throwing skills in the context of a pass or shot on goal in basketball, team handball, and so on. The reference used to define the vertical plane is the axis of the shoulder.

Depending upon the posture that a player uses, he or she may achieve throws that differ in terms of length and shape. One critical rule: The longer the desired shot, the more important the required throwing path. This is shown in Figure 6.16.

For players, it is important to understand that the capacity to produce a long throw is an asset for the ball carrier. In fact, in games where the ball is handled with the hands, players are quick to identify the kind

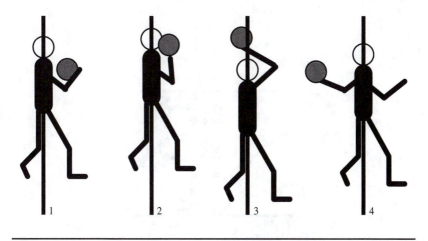

Fig. 6.15 Players' postures with reference to hand throwing.

of posture used by the throwing player and thus to foresee where the ball is likely to be thrown. The main postures that one can see on the playing surface are illustrated in Figure 6.17 along with the different shapes of the ball trajectory and related estimated distances.

If we combine the manipulation range in relation to the upper body with players' postures with reference to throwing, we obtain an excellent frame of reference for analyzing the capacities of the player in possession of the ball.

Players' location on the field at the time of throw-ins is in direct connection with the estimated thrower's capacity, and this yields different

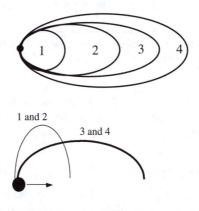

Fig. 6.16 Lengths and shapes of throws according to the postures illustrated in Figure 6.15.

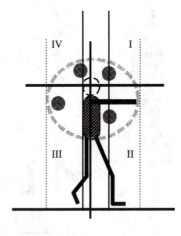

Fig. 6.17 An illustration of the manipulation range in relation to the upper body.

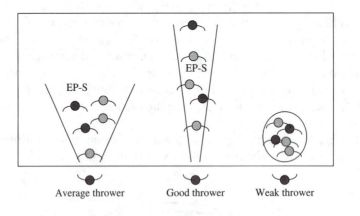

Fig. 6.18 Effective play-space in relation to a player's throwing capacities in restarting a game of soccer, basketball, handball, and so on.

effective play-spaces. Figure 6.18 illustrates the results obtained in a basketball experiment conducted at the Department of Physical Education in Dijon (Gréhaigne, Billard, Laroche, 1999).

Exchanging the Ball with Growing Complexity

Various ways of exchanging the ball are also elements that one must carefully observe because they yield accurate information on the level of play in a given force ratio. From the easiest to the most difficult ball

Face to face

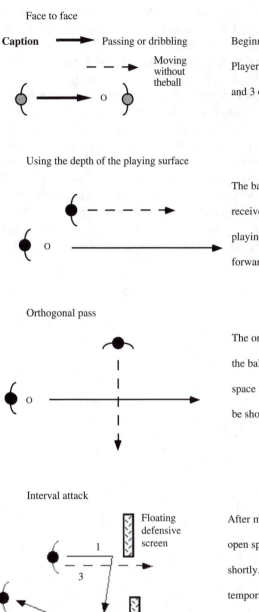

Caption ──────▶ Passing or dribbling

― ― ▶ Moving without the ball

Beginners' classical positioning:

Players are generally face to face, still, and 3 or 4 meters apart.

Using the depth of the playing surface

The ball carrier is still and the intended receiver is running in the depth of the playing surface. The ball is passed forward in the player's running axis.

Orthogonal pass

The orthogonal pass consists in passing the ball at the right time in an open space where the intended receiver will be shortly.

Interval attack

Floating defensive screen

After moving the ball, it is thrown in an open space where the player will be shortly. This requires an accurate temporal adjustment.

Fig. 6.19 Exchanging the ball with growing complexity.

exchange, we will examine some features: speed, location, and the direction of a player's movement according to the movements of the ball. These analyses are shown in Figure 6.19.

The analysis of players' paths, ball trajectories, and ball circulation constitutes valuable indicators for obtaining information about the actual play level and its evolution from previous matches or lessons.

In a physical education school setting, teachers and student observers collect information based on personal observations and will interpret reality according to a personal frame of reference (Gréhaigne, Godbout, & Bouthier, 2001). The role of the teacher is to provide feedback to students, describing and explaining the players' actions. Based on qualitative or quantitative indicators, the teacher favors the connection between objective data collected by observers and the result of the action. In the next two chapters we will examine the assessment of game performance and its role in the teaching-learning process of sport-related games.

7

PERFORMANCE ASSESSMENT
IN TEAM SPORTS

The first element that comes to mind when one considers the analysis of a player's performance concerns his or her ability to apply motor responses to the resolution of game play problems. This notion limits a player's knowledge of typical skills and behaviors that are organized and presented based on their difficulty from simple to complex. Based on our explanation of the different components that constitute game play, the assessment of a player's performance provides a broader view. Game performance must be accomplished in a real life context and must reflect the different components that are important to a team's performance. The instruments presented in chapter 6 offer teachers and coaches a qualitative approach for the analysis of a team or an individual's play based on selected criteria.

In the current chapter, we will present different assessment strategies that can be used in the analysis of game components, either on a team or at the individual level. Also, we will examine in more detail the particular contexts and challenges of assessing performance in a team sport setting. The assessment strategies discussed in this chapter will then lead us to the description and explanation of two assessment instruments examines an individual's global performance. These two instruments will be presented in chapter 8.

PERFORMANCE ASSESSMENT IN TEAM SPORTS

There appears to be agreement among researchers in sport pedagogy as to the importance of authentic assessment in the teaching-learning process of team sports. As showed by Veal (1988); Cardinet (1986); and Allal, Cardinet, and Perrenoud (1985), assessment can take the form of preassessment, formative assessment, or summative assessment depending upon the phase at which it occurs and the reason for which it is implemented. If assessment is to be truly integrated with the teaching-learning process, it must meet at least two requirements. The first is ecological validity (Gardner, 1992), which refers to the relationship of measurement with what is taught and to the fact that the assessment is done in context so that it does not disturb the normal functioning of the classroom. The second requirement is the active participation of students in assessment as it is integrated into the teaching-learning process (Wiggins, 1993; Zessoules & Gardner, 1991).

Thus, problems with the assessment of any given player in team sports are those related to the assessment of any complex system, that is, the intervening elements are not only numerous but also interacting; the force ratio plays an important role, and it may vary in different opposition situations or even during one given situation; the interdependence of the members of a given team; and the assessment of a single player within a coherent system (that is, within the team).

FACETS OF PERFORMANCE ASSESSMENT IN TEAM SPORTS

Authentic assessment of performance in team sports offers a special challenge to physical education teachers and coaches. Beyond the usual motor fitness components, it is generally agreed that performance in team sports results from the interaction of strategy efficiency, tactical efficiency, and specific perceptual and motor skills (Gréhaigne & Godbout, 1995). In an effort to take into account the various facets likely to be of concern in the assessment of motor performance, Godbout (1990) has proposed a two-dimensional model (see Figure 7.1) that leads to the identification of four general categories of information or objects of measurement. All four categories of information may be considered to be of interest in the case of team sports performance assessment. On the one hand the model recognizes that an assessor may wish to consider the technical aspects or the tactical aspects of a player's performance. On the other hand the assessment may be focused on the result or the end product of the player's actions or on the way those actions are conducted, (the process). The distinction between product and process with reference to the assessment of motor skills has been briefly explained by Brown (1982) and has been described in greater details by Veal (1995) and may apply to the tactical aspects of sport performance (Werner, Thorpe, & Bunker, 1996). It may also be associated with the notions of *knowledge of results* (KR) and *knowledge of performance* (KP) used by motor learning researchers with reference to augmented or extrinsic feedback (Schmidt, 1991). Combining both technique versus tactics and product versus process, one can identify four facets of performance assessment in team sports:

1. Information relative to a *technical product*: For instance, is the player able to reach a partner when passing the ball?
2. Information relative to a *technical process*: For instance, how does the player proceed to pass the ball?
3. Information relative to a *tactical product*: For instance, player B is responsible for covering player C; does player C manage to receive a pass anyway or does player B effectively succeed in eliminating player C from the play?
4. Information relative to a tactical process: For instance, how does player B proceed to cover player C and prevent him or her from receiving a pass?

Figure 7.1 illustrates these facets of performance.

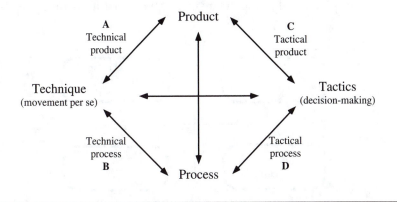

Fig. 7.1 Facets involved in the assessment of performance in team sports (Godbout, 1990).

CURRENT ASSESSMENT PRACTICES IN TEAM SPORTS

To collect information relative to these facets of performance, physical education teachers and coaches have developed various measurement strategies. In an attempt to summarize these practices, Godbout (1990) has proposed the two-dimensional model illustrated in Figure 7.2. On one hand, the model recognizes that in some instances the measurements are done in standardized set-ups, whereas in other cases, the information is collected in real life situations (that is, during regular matches). On the other hand, the measurement procedure may be quantitative in nature (low inference), relying on physical units of measurement, or it may be qualitative (high inference), relying on the use of rating instruments. By combining both dimensions of the model, one can identify four general strategies for collecting information with regard to a player's performance in team sports:

1. **Standardized tests.** For instance, asking a student to shoot a basketball into a basket as many times as possible over 20 trials from a given position.
2. **Statistics derived from competition.** For instance, computing the average number of controlled rebounds over a certain number of games.
3. **The rating of performance in standardized set-ups.** For instance, having every student execute five volleyball or tennis serves on an empty court and rating the quality or form of the serves.
4. **The rating of performance during the game.** For instance, observing a player during a match and rating the way he or she proceeds to penetrate in the scoring zone or observing a defensive player and rating the quality of his or her individual defense.

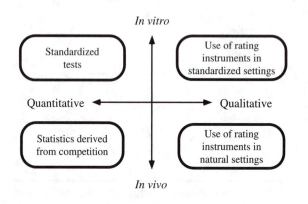

Fig. 7.2 Measurement strategies for assessing performance in team sports (Godbout, 1990).

Whether one consults Barrow, McGee, and Tritschler (1989), Baumgartner and Jackson (1991), McGee (1984), Safrit and Wood (1995), or any other measurement and evaluation textbooks in physical education, there is little doubt that testing efforts related to team sport performance have been focused on standardized tests. Typically, with reference to the model presented in Figure 7.2, such tests are focused on the *technical product* aspect of the student's performance. Without necessarily using published standardized tests, teachers do use similar homemade skill tests (Desrosiers, Genet-Volet, & Godbout, 1997; Veal, 1992). Although not widely used by teachers in physical education classes, observational instruments have been devised by coaches to register the frequency or number of various events occurring during a match (that is, the number of goals, penalties, percentage of successful shots, etc.). Such statistics focus on the result of performance. It is, however, impossible to determine whether these statistics reflect the technical aspect of performance, its tactical aspect, or both.

Over the last 15 years, there has been a growing interest in assessment procedures that address the process aspect of performance. Pinheiro's (1994) work illustrates the use of rating scales to assess the quality of motor skills; they may be used in standardized set-ups or in game contexts as well. McGee (1984) has provided examples of rating scales used to assess the tactical performance of children during games. More recently two authentic assessment instruments have been designed, the Game Performance Assessment Instrument (GPAI) (Griffin, Mitchell & Oslin, 1997; Oslin, Mitchell & Griffin, 1998) and the Team Sport Assessment Procedure (TSAP) (Gréhaigne, Godbout & Bouthier, 1997) to provide researchers, teachers and students with a means of observing and coding performance behaviors in game play context. Observations of secondary physical education teachers' assessment practices nevertheless show that some of them do consider tactical aspects of game play in teacher-made assessment instruments (Desrosiers et al., 1997). The work accomplished by Mitchell and his colleagues (Mitchell, Griffin, & Oslin, 1994; Mitchell, Oslin, & Griffin, 1995; Oslin, Mitchell, & Griffin, 1998), the University of South Carolina Group (Taylor et al., reported by Werner et al., 1996) and Blomquist and colleagues work with game-understanding test procedures (Blomquist et al., 2000) is an indication of a growing interest in this area.

Deciding what aspect of a given team sport ought to be assessed depends upon teachers' views as to what students should learn. As pointed out by Bailey & Almond (1983), Gréhaigne & Godbout (1995), Turner & Martinek (1995), and Werner et al. (1996), it is common in the teaching of team sports for teachers to start by working on a series of technical skills; then, when these skills appear to be reasonably mastered, more emphasis is put on playing the game and on related tactical skills. Such an approach to teaching team sports leads to motor skill–oriented assessment practices. It has been suggested by Mahlo (1974); Bouthier (1988); Bunker & Thorpe (1986); Turner & Martinek (1995); Gréhaigne, Billard, & Laroche (1999); and Butler, Griffin, Lombardo, & Nastasi (2003) that a greater emphasis should be put sooner in the learning process on understanding the game and on tactical efficiency. Such an approach would then make it all the more important to consider strategic and tactical efficiency in an assessment procedure.

USING NUMERICAL INDICES FOR FORMATIVE ASSESSMENT PURPOSES

If we return to the notion of formative and authentic assessment presented earlier in this chapter, we realize that these assessment characteristics are very important to a player's construction of team sports knowledge and skills. In education as a whole, there is also this growing interest for authentic formative assessment. This does not mean that we are now dealing with a new kind of formative assessment; the connotation of "authenticity" is intended to put the focus on the central nature and purpose of formative assessment (Allal, Cardinet, & Perrenoud, 1979). In 1992, Veal presented the main characteristics of authentic assessment in connection with physical education and sport:

a) "… it is regular and ongoing …

b) … [there is] a connection between daily instructional tasks and assessment …

c) … the teacher can 'see the skill' that is being evaluated, and there is a connection between skills and real-life situations as learning indicators …

d) … it accounts for student effort, improvement, and participation." (p. 90)

Formative Assessment and the Teaching-Learning Process

Formative assessment must be seen as a complement to teaching and coaching; it is and must be understood as an essential part of the teaching-learning process. Thus, if it is to be implemented, teachers must include the following steps in their teaching procedures:

1. **Communication of expectations.** Before getting into practice, players should know what it is they are trying to achieve. At what

point, expressed in concrete terms, can they consider that they have mastered the learning objective? This goes beyond stating the general objective and describing the learning task for them; unless they are given some type of success criteria, students will never know by themselves whether they have succeeded.

2. **Collection of information.** At some point during practice, players should know whether they have succeeded. Thus information regarding their performance must be collected either formally or informally. This can be done through observation by the teacher or peers, through self-assessment (with or without observational grids or through questionnaires), and so on. The idea is to get information that can be interpreted in light of the expectations or success criteria put forward by the teacher or even initially selected by the students themselves.

3. **Regulation of learning.** Only a few students succeed on their first trial. The real challenge and one wonders whether they need teaching at all. The true challenge of teaching is the management of success and failure. What is the use of telling students they have not succeeded if one does not do anything about it? A regulation scenario often used by teachers consists of providing students with feedback and then having them resume practice. The teacher may also encourage the students to put forward hypotheses for solving some tactical or motor problem, either through teacher-guided discussions (Rauschenbach, 1996), free discussions within teams, individual questioning, and so on. Other types of regulation scenarios may include an adaptation of learning tasks; going over an earlier, insufficiently mastered learning task; and so on.

The regulation of learning, which is a process that teachers rightly associate with teaching, requires that some information be obtained to start with, but getting information is not sufficient. Indeed, any collected information that does not help the teacher and students make decisions remains worthless as far as learning is concerned. This is why formative assessment cannot really be considered separately from teaching. It follows that a discussion about formative assessment cannot ignore the underlying teaching-learning process.

Authentic Formative Assessment in Team Sports

Authentic assessment of performance in team sports offers a special challenge to physical education teachers and coaches. For the information to be useful, it must be collected in real life situations. To accomplish this, French sport pedagogy researchers tried out various procedures to assess game play in context. The basic idea was to take into account players' specific behaviors during the game and to summarize the information through numerical data. In some cases, the final result takes the form of a score attributed to the team as a whole (for example, the number of times the team got possession of the ball); in other cases, the observation focuses on individual players' performance.

Assessment Indices

On the basis of objective data, students construct and learn tactical knowledge in relationship to motor skills. As discussed by Gréhaigne (1992), tactics relate to a) the effective positions taken in reaction to an opponent in a game situation and b) the adaptation or flexibility of the team to the conditions of play. Tactics are therefore momentary adaptations to new configurations of play (that is, the particular distribution of the players and moving of the ball on the field at given moments) and to the circulation of the ball; they are adaptations to opposition. Numerical data make it possible to examine the outcome of such tactics. When mastered, the problem solving of configurations of play indicates that tactical knowledge learning that is linked to motor skills is taking place.

To understand the progress students are making in terms of tactical skills and the offensive efficiency of each team, the teacher and students should register certain significant occurrences seen as indicators of an adaptation to problems brought about by the configurations of play (Mérand, 1984). The following sections discuss some occurrences that could be used on a collective or individual basis in various team sports.

Team Indices Teachers and coaches should focus the students' attention on three combined team indices throughout a match: number of possessions of the ball, number of shots, and number of goals. When recorded during intervals ranging from 7 to 14 minutes in short matches involving balanced teams, each one of those parameters will yield valuable formative information to each team, to each student, and to the teacher. For instance, a greater number of possessions of the ball as compared to that of a previous match, or a greater number of shots for the same number of possessions, will indicate collective progress on the part of the students. A simple data sheet can be used by each team to compare information relative to the indices (see Figure 7.3).

Again in relation to ball possession, in high-level soccer, a team gains possession of the ball between 100 and 110 times during a 90-minute match. In a school physical education setting, experiments by Gréhaigne et al. and Richard et al. have been conducted using 7-minute observation periods. In such a time frame, a team typically gains possession of the ball 12 times (± 1). In the context of European handball, between 16 and 18 ball possessions (± 1) have been observed with 12–16-year-old students.

It should be noted that the difference of ball possessions between the two teams can never be larger than one. This is a simple way to verify whether the student observers did their job correctly. For a basketball team after a 7-minute match, a total of 20 possessions of the ball resulting in four shots and one goal shows too large a number of lost balls. The students can be asked to solve this problem before worrying about improving their shooting skills.

Team _____ Match _____		
Indices	Occurences	Total
Possessions of the ball		
Shots		
Goals		

Fig. 7.3   Data sheet for each team (translation from Gréhaigne, 1992).

For more complex assessment situations, including time constraints or a smaller playing surface combined with a larger number of players in reference to the principle of "playing in movement," all one needs is to tally the number of positive responses after a player has gained possession of the ball. For example, three positive responses—either passes or shots on the goal—out of 12 played balls is sufficient to observe a transformation in a player's behavior.

Yet another way of obtaining game play data in a small-sided game context is to analyze game play sequences (Dugrand, 1989). These sequences are defined as the ball is exchanged among teammates from the time they gain possession of the ball to the time they lose it. In this assessment context, we note all ball exchanges within a team and we also note which players are putting the ball back into play and which are taking free or penalty kicks (or throws and shots in basketball, handball, etc.).

Game play sequences provide important information like the number of ball exchanges and ball possessions within a certain time frame. The former number is often linked to the confrontational level. We can also detect who is putting the ball back into play, who is giving the ball away to the opposition, and so on. It is also possible to construct a graph of all the exchanges to illustrate player relations and consequently to obtain a graphic representation of the competency rapport and the typical ball circulation that exists within a team when facing a given type of opposition.

Single-Player Indices For individual players, one can note some numerical data that are indicative of their adaptation to the opposition encountered. The use of some or all of the following indices can be very useful.

Figure 7.4 presents an observational grid that can be used to register one or many performance indices. While planning formative assessment, the teacher can choose one or several indicators, depending upon the feedback that he or she wants to put at the children's disposal. For instance, a teacher may have the students analyze their number of played balls (PB), conquered balls (CB), and lost balls (LB). For an equal PB result of 18, two students should come to very different conclusions if one has 7 CB and 2 LB while the other has 1 CB and 9 LB. The first one brings the ball to the team while the latter loses it 50% of the time (9 lost balls for 18 played balls). If both students belong to the same team, it is a problem to be solved within the team. Thus, once the assessment results are communicated, each player and each team is faced with problems of some sort: how to reduce the number of lost balls and increase the number of shots, how to improve the movement of the ball, what strategy to adopt, and so on.

The Volume of Play Another way to envision this assessment problem consists of analyzing the volume of play. This analysis is based on the postulate that in the context of a small-sided game, the more a player is in contact with the ball, the more he or she is involved in the game, and the more he or she participates in a team's performance.

The volume of play expresses a player or a team's involvement in the game and takes into account the force ratio. As expressed earlier, the volume of play is defined simply as the number of balls played by an individual or a team. It is not a coincidence if a player receives or conquers the ball frequently or infrequently. His or her availability, tactical ability, and fatigue level depend directly upon his or her game play intelligence and ability to communicate with teammates. As previously explained, when a teacher respects the principle of balance, the notion

Elements assessed	Criteria	Name : —————— Team : —————— Match : ——————		
Availability during play	Received balls (RB)	1st half	2nd half	Total
Defensive capacities	Conquered ball (CB)			
Offensive capacities	Passess to the partner (PP)			
	Shots (S)			
	Goals (G)			
Adaptation to the play	Lost balls (LB)			
Volume of play	Total number of played balls (PB) = (RB+CB)			

Fig. 7.4 Example of data sheet for a player (translation from Gréhaigne, 1992).

of game intensity can be assessed by computing the number of played balls by both teams (Gréhaigne, 1989; 1992).

An Illustration of Assessment Using the Volume of Play Through different work accomplished with physical education classes, Gréhaigne (1995) has looked at the number of played balls in 5 vs. 5 soccer (4 players + 1 goalkeeper). The analyzed matches were played on a 50 m × 30 m field with 6 m × 2 m goals. Pertaining to specific rules, there is no offside, throw-ins are done with the feet, and corners are done by hand. During the matches, student observers tallied the number of played balls for each of the players on the field.

The students involved in this project were 36 graduating high school (*Lycée*) students (17–18 years old). Eight teams of four players were formed, and a three-game tournament was played. The extra players served as observers or goalkeepers.

First of all, we will take a look at the number of balls played by each team (Table 7.1), and then we will analyze the repartition of balls within each team (Table 7.2).

TABLE 7.1 Total of Played Balls per Game Between Two Teams

A1- B1 = 152	E2 - G2 = 130
C1 - D1= 172	F2 - H2 = 161
E1 - F1 = 137	A3 - D3 = 171
G1 - H1 = 152	B3 - C3 = 134
A2 - C2 = 149	E3 - H3 = 138
B2 - D2 = 169	F3 - G3 = 143

In matches where teams played more than 160 balls in a 14-minute time frame (2×7-minute halves), it was noticed that play was fast, leading up to many shots on goal situations. A game at this intensity level reflected a high skill level (i.e., one-touch passing). Teams playing around 140 balls a match reflected slower play, often characterized by one or two players keeping possession of the ball. Weaker teams seemed to be playing around the 120-ball level. These teams' play was characterized by numerous balls lost to opponents.

The number of played balls is not necessarily divided by half between the confronted teams. Hence, we can compare the number of played balls to the final score. Team C1 (Table 7.1) played 82 balls and won 2–1, even though team D1 played 90 balls. Team F3 played 78 balls and easily won 5–2 against G3, who played 65 balls.

During a match, one can also study the way teammates exchange the ball. In the current sample of students, we observed the following

TABLE 7.2 Ball Possessions Among Individuals Players Across Teams

Team	P1	P2	P3	P4	Total	Team	P1	P2	P3	P4	Total
A1	21	26	21	14	**82**	E1	15	19	15	12	**61**
A2	22	20	16	17	**75**	E2	19	15	10	15	**59**
A3	28	19	21	15	**83**	E3	18	14	15	16	**63**
B1	22	11	14	23	**70**	F1	22	24	12	18	**76**
B2	20	12	24	12	**68**	F2	21	20	17	25	**83**
B3	20	11	20	13	**64**	F3	22	14	18	24	**78**
C1	22	20	25	15	**82**	G1	12	13	20	19	**64**
C2	17	13	27	17	**74**	G2	15	20	15	21	**71**
C3	16	23	17	14	**70**	G3	11	12	22	20	**65**
D1	17	24	25	24	**90**	H1	16	19	23	30	**88**
D2	25	24	18	34	**101**	H2	24	16	19	19	**78**
D3	21	20	20	27	**88**	H3	27	15	18	15	**75**

breakdown with teams that played more than 80 balls: team leader: 25–30 balls; players 2 and 3: 19–24 balls; worst player: approximately 15 balls. In the game in which there were 101 played balls (team D-1), the same ratio of played balls was observed (34; 25–24; 18). In the rest of the matches of different intensity levels, there was always at least one player who dominated play, while two others were involved moderately, and one seemed to be weaker than the rest.

Figure 7.5 illustrates that to obtain clear and reliable information, one must compute a team's number of played balls both collectively and individually. Two distribution percentages can effectively represent very different realities in terms of game play performance.

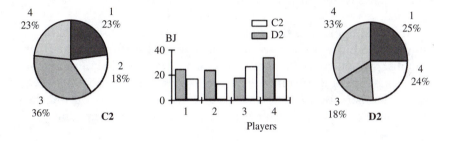

Fig. 7.5 Number of played balls for teams C2 and D2.

The use of these numerical data based on certain components of game play is not to be taken as a universal approach. This assessment strategy is based on a holistic approach to better analyze the end results in an opposition relationship. To be used effectively, statistical transformation of raw data is often required. From this transformation, tables and graphics can be constructed for a specific population. This type of data can also help to determine player difficulties or lack of comprehension pertaining to game concepts.

If a team played 80 balls during a match, one can formally analyze a match by decomposing how each teammate contributed to the outcome of the game. The following breakdowns exemplify possible scenarios:

a. 38 played balls for the best player, 17 and 17 for players 2 and 3, and 8 for the weakest player
b. 31 played balls for each of the two best players and 9 played balls for each of the two weakest players
c. 23 played balls for each of the two best players and 18 played balls for each of the two other players

One or two players seem to be dominant in this 4 vs. 4 game structure. Globally, the results that emerged from this experiment provide valuable information on the competency and rapport within a team. In a context where teams were divided in a random fashion, it was noticed that 90 played balls in a 14-minute time frame was a good result, and playing less than 60 balls was considered a weak performance. With a result of approximately 70 balls, another variable must be taken into consideration to better discriminate performance among teams: this variable is the number of shots on goal.

Game play behaviors can vary among players due to external factors (e.g., size of playing surface) and the team sport being played. This ensemble of behaviors and the variability associated with them are what makes team sports didactics in a physical education context so original.

To better appreciate the participation and accomplishments of all students within a group, a teacher can choose a game component that can discriminate performance to obtain an interesting photograph of what is happening within a team and the existing rapport between team members. Beyond the notions of played balls and shots on goal mentioned earlier, other game play variables can be used for game play assessment:

Exploited balls = Played balls – Lost balls

Neutral balls = Exploited balls – Attack balls (Passes, Shots on goal, so on)

These variables and indices represent interesting ways of assessing performance. However, they must be verified and refined to develop an objective strategy of assessing team sport performance.

LEARNING TO OBSERVE

Watching game play and observing specific students' behaviors are two different things. Students must learn to observe and focus their attention on specific occurrences during a match, sometimes sharing satisfaction or frustration with teammates but never forgetting to register whatever information they are supposed to collect.

Observational training should start with team indices. They are easier to register since there is no need to discriminate among players of the same team. Depending on whether teams are made up of several players playing on rotation or fewer players playing all the time, observers will be teammates not involved in game play or players of another team not involved in a particular match. At first, each of the three team performance variables may be observed by a different student, but eventually a single student can take charge of two and then of all three variables. Also, more than one student may be asked to assume the same task, with the possibility of comparing notes at the end of the period of play. Another way of familiarizing students with the observational task is called the "reporter game" (Dugrand, 1985) and has been used with students as young as eight years old (Gréhaigne & Guillon, 1990). In the reporter game, one student observes both teams involved in game play and describes the action as someone on the radio would. Another student plays the role of the reporter's secretary, registering the information provided by the reporter under the appropriate form, usually a team performance occurrence (e.g., possession of ball, shot, goal, etc.). Variations of the reporter game may call for a reporter and secretary to be assigned to each team, or two secretaries to be assigned to one reporter and having to compare notes, and so on. Also, at times teachers will involve students who attend the physical education class but cannot participate in the game because of injuries or health problems.

Once students are familiar with the observation of team indices, teachers may gradually introduce observations focused on single players. To do that, simply have as many observers as there are players involved in the game, which means dividing the class group into an even number of balanced teams and pairing students, with members of each pair assuming in turn the roles of player and observer. Observers lacking attention will soon realize that the players they are paired with often keep count of their own behaviors and are willing to question false results. When student observers are focused on single players' performance, the teacher should make sure that the teams involved in game play are not only balanced but also stable; if there is a rotation of players, results may be misleading since players are likely to spend different lengths of time on the court.

Finally, one important aspect for the teacher to remember while introducing students to peer observation is to make it clear from the start that their involvement in such observational tasks does not mean that they are doing the teacher's work. Far from that, it means that they are learning to take charge of their game and that, while observing, they are also reflecting on the requirements of the game.

In the first part of our exploration on assessment practices in a team-sport setting, we have presented some philosophical and theoretical notions as well as practical assessments related to the whole team's performance. In chapter 8, we will present two assessment instruments developed for the assessment of a player's individual performance.

8

AN INTRODUCTION TO THE TEAM-SPORT ASSESSMENT PROCEDURE AND THE GAME PERFORMANCE ASSESSMENT INSTRUMENT

In this chapter we continue to address the role of assessment in the teaching and learning of sport-related games. When implementing a tactical games model (i.e., game sense, conceptual-based games, TGfU) the teachers' goal for students is to focus on successful game play, which means that assessment should focus on game play (Veal, 1992). In other words, if the goal of games teaching is to improve game performance, then it is essential that assessment measures take into consideration two critical components. First, assessment measures should consist of all aspects of performance. A player's game performance includes concepts related to tactical awareness and understanding (i.e., what to do?) and skill execution (how to do it?). Second, assessment needs to measure game play in context (i.e., actual games or game forms).

Currently, when physical education teachers assess, they rely on skill testing to assess student performance. Using skill tests to assess game performance is problematic for several reasons: (a) skill tests do not predict playing performance; (b) skill tests do not take into account the social dimensions of sport-related games; (c) skill tests are out of context in situations not related to game play; and (d) skills test do not reflect a broader view of game performance (Griffin, Mitchell, & Oslin, 1997; Oslin, Mitchell, & Griffin, 1998). Two assessment instruments, the Team Sport Assessment Procedure (TSAP) and the Game Performance Assessment Instrument (GPAI), have been designed and validated to assess players' individuals performance in real-life learning scenarios—the game. The purpose of this chapter is twofold. First, we will introduce the major features of the TSAP and the GPAI. Second, we will provide the pedagogical and practical implications for using the instruments in sport-related teaching and learning.

THE TEAM SPORT ASSESSMENT PROCEDURE (TSAP)

The Team Sport Assessment Procedure (TSAP) was developed by Gréhaigne, Godbout, and Bouthier (1997). It provides information that quantifies an individual's overall offensive performance in selected invasion sports, such as basketball, soccer, and so on, and in net team sports, such as volleyball. It reflects both technical and tactical aspects of game play (Gréhaigne et al., 1997). The information provided by the individual variables, performance indices, and performance score are all macroindicators of both technical and tactical performance (Table 8.1). These indicators are all related to successful game play (Gréhaigne et al., 1997).

TABLE 8.1 The Relationships Between Observation Items and Types of Information Collected

Observation Items	Information Collected
Received balls (RB)	Involvement of the player in the team's play (availability, accessibility to receive a pass)
Conquered balls (CB)	Information related to the player's defensive capacities
Offensive balls (OB)	Player's capacity to make significant passes to his or her partners (offensive capacities)
Successful shots (SS)	Information related to the player's offensive capacities
Volume of play (PB = RB + CB)	General involvement of the player in the game
Lost balls (LB)	A small number reflects a good adaptation to the game

Source: Gréhaigne, Godbout, & Bouthier, 1997.

The TSAP is based on two basic notions: (a) "How a player gains possession of the ball" (2 variables) and (b) "How a player disposes of the ball" (4 variables). According to these notions a player's specific behaviors are observed and coded during game play on an observation grid such as the one presented in Figure 8.1. Two performance indices and a performance score are then computed from the collected data (Table 8.2).

Team Sport Assessment Procedure for Invasion Games

Name _____

                Class _____

Observer _____

                Date _____

Directions: Observe student's game play and place a tally mark in the appropriate box.

Gaining possession of the ball

Played Balls (PB)

Conquered Ball (CB)   Received Ball (RB)

Disposing of the ball

Lost Ball (LB)	Neutral Ball (NB)	Pass (P)	Successful Shot (SS)

Fig. 8.1 Observation grid for the TSAP – Invasion games.

A primary feature of the TSAP is that the data collection process is accomplished by students. A recent study demonstrated that students as young as 10 years old (grade 5) were capable of using the TSAP with a good deal of precision and reliability (Richard, Godbout, & Gréhaigne, 2000). The use of this assessment procedure combined with a TGfU model can offer an efficient means to develop students' learning of game concepts (Gréhaigne & Godbout, 1998).

TABLE 8.2 Observational Variables, Performance Indices, and Performance Score Computation Formula for the Team Sport Assessment Procedure—Invasion Games

Observational Variables: Operational Definition

A. Gaining possession of the ball

1. Conquered Ball (CB)

A player is considered to have conquered the ball if he or she intercepted it, stole it from an opponent, or recaptured it after an unsuccessful shot on goal or after a near loss to the other team.

2. Received Ball (RB)

The player receives the ball from a partner and does not immediately lose control of it.

B. Disposing of the ball

1. Lost Ball (LB)

The player is considered to have lost the ball when he or she loses control of it without having scored a goal.

2. Neutral Ball (NB)

A routine pass to a partner who does not truly put pressure on the other team.

3. Pass (P)

Pass to a partner that contributes to the displacement of the ball towards the opposing team's goal.

4. Successful Shot on Goal (SS)

A shot is considered successful when it scores or possession of the ball is retained by one's team.

The computation of performance indices and performance score:

Volume of play index = CB + RB

$$\text{Efficiency Index (EI)} = \frac{\text{VP}}{10 + \text{LB}}$$

Performance score = (volume of play/2) + (efficiency index × 10)

Source: Gréhaigne, Godbout, & Bouthier, 1997.

Using the TSAP in Sport-Related Teaching and Learning

A major feature of the TSAP is its adaptability to different teaching scenarios. What has been explained up to this point is a procedure that possesses six different observational variables that have been shown to reflect a student's global offensive performance in invasion games. When teaching more complex tactical problems at a higher grade level—for example, high school—the integral version of the TSAP is recommended. A teacher might, however, not want to use the integral version of the TSAP if the learning outcomes he or she is pursuing do not require such a complex procedure (i.e., upper elementary and middle school programs) or if, not having experimented with peer assessment very much, a teacher might feel that the students would need to be initiated with a simpler instrument. These are legitimate concerns, as observational complexity and cognitive maturity are definitely factors that need to be considered when integrating students in the peer assessment process. With regard to the use of the TSAP, Richard, Godbout, and Picard (2000) have developed, experimented with, and validated simpler versions of the TSAP to offer teachers alternatives for their assessment practices in relation to games education. The following pages offer a rationale for these modified versions in relation to their use in games education at lower grade levels (i.e., grades 5 to 8). For the purpose of this book, the TSAP will be presented pertaining to its use in relation to invasion games.

Invasion Games: 1st Modified Version

Volume of Play (VP) = # of possessions Conquered Ball (CB) + Received Ball (RB)

$$\text{Efficiency Index (EI)} = \frac{VP}{10 + LB}$$

Performance Score $= (VP/2) + (EI \times 10)$

In this first modified version, the number of observational variables is reduced by half. With regard to the volume of play, no distinction is made between CB or RB. Only the total number of possessions is taken into consideration along with the number of lost balls. The reasoning behind this decision is twofold. First, we have noticed through different experiments with the TSAP that younger observers have a tendency to indicate most ball possessions as received, even if they are conquered or intercepted. Second, the nuance between these two variables are not so important in relation to game concepts taught at the lower grade levels.

The modified version of the TSAP is simpler than the original version. The modifications permit teachers to progressively integrate students in the observation of game play behavior without having an overly complex instrument to use. Also, the variables that were retained for this first modified version allow teachers and students to still make nuances about game play concepts such as getting away from a defender (represented by the volume of play) or ball circulation, which are mostly taught at the upper elementary level (grades 5 and 6) in most physical education programs. Through the efficiency index, we want students to realize that from their volume of play—the number of possessions—the goal is to lose as few balls as possible, which reflects a good contribution to team success whether it be passing the ball or shooting on goal.

Invasion Games: 2nd Modified Version

Volume of Play (VP) = # of possessions (CB + RB)

$$\text{Efficiency Index (EI)} = \frac{\text{Pass} + \text{Successful Shot}}{10 + \text{LB}}$$

Performance score = (VP/2) + (EI × 10)

Like the first modified version, this second version lets the teacher put a certain pedagogical emphasis in relation to the lesson objectives. In this case, the efficiency index's numerator is composed of the number of passes and successful shots on goal. In this version the pedagogical emphasis is on both gaining possession of and disposing of the ball in a successful manner (e.g., pass to teammate or shot on goal). The efficiency index helps the teacher guide the student to know whether he or she should pass the ball or shoot on goal. This second modified version of the TSAP increases the number of observational variables to four. Consequently, this second version could be considered an intermediate version of the original TSAP.

THE GAME PERFORMANCE ASSESSMENT INSTRUMENT (GPAI)

The Game Performance Assessment Instrument was developed to be a comprehensive assessment tool for teachers to use and adapt in assessing a variety of games. Teachers can use the GPAI for different types of games across the classification system (e.g., invasion, net/wall) or within a particular classification (e.g., basketball, soccer). The different observational variables included in the GPAI permit the coding of behaviors that demonstrate the ability to solve tactical problems in games by making decisions, moving appropriately (off-the-ball movement), and executing skills (Griffin et al., 1997).

Seven observable game components have been identified and formulated in the initial development of the GPAI (Oslin, Mitchell, & Griffin, 1998). These are shown in Table 8.3. Game components can be coded on observation grids (see Figure 8.2). All components are related to game performance, but not all of the seven components are applicable to a particular game (Oslin et al., 1998). For example, all components except "guard" are important for field/run/score/games, such as softball. On the other hand, all components except "base" are important for successful soccer performance (Oslin et al., 1998).

TABLE 8.3 Components of Game Performance

Base	Appropriate return of performer to a recovery (base) position between skill attempts
Decision-Making	Makes appropriate decisions about what to do with the ball (or projectile) during a game
Skill Execution	Efficient execution of selected skills
Support	Provides appropriate support for a teammate with the ball (or projectile) by being in position to receive a pass
Guard/Mark	Appropriate guarding/marking of an opponent who may or may not have the ball (or projectile)
Cover	Provides appropriate defensive cover, help, or backup for a player making a challenge for the ball (or projectile)
Adjust	Movement of performer, either offensively or defensively, as necessitated by the flow of the game

Reprinted, by permission, from Griffin, Mitchell, & Oslin, 1997, p. 220.

The GPAI was designed to be a flexible observation instrument that can be used to assess students' performance either in a live setting or from videotapes. Teachers can choose to observe any or all components related to a particular game, depending on the context of the instructional environment (Oslin et al., 1998). Simplification of the GPAI in the number and particular components to be observed is especially useful when students are involved in peer assessment.

The GPAI has been shown to be a valid assessment instrument. Content, construct, and ecological validity have all been established during its preliminary development (Oslin et al., 1998). Furthermore, instrument and observer reliability have also been established (Oslin et al., 1998).

Using the GPAI in Sport-Related Teaching and Learning

The appeal of the GPAI is that teachers can adapt the instrument for use based on the aspects of the game taught and the type of game being played. There are two basic scoring methods for using the GPAI: (a) the 1–5 scoring system (see Figure 8.2) and (b) the tally scoring system (see Figure 8.3).

Game Performance Assessment Instrument
Invasion Games

Class_____   Evaluator_____ Team_____ Game

_____

Observation Dates (a) _____ (b) _____ (c) _____ (d) _____

Scoring Key: 5 = Very effective performance

                      4 = Effective performance

                      3 = Moderately effective performance

                      2 = Weak performance

                      1 = Very weak performance

Components/Criteria

   1. Decision made—

      a. Student attempts to pass to an open teammate

      b. Student attempts to shoot when appropriate

   2. Skill Execution—

      a. Reception—control pass

      b. Pass—ball reaches intended target

      c. Dribble—control and adjust and move position

   3. Support—

      a. Students attempt to move into position to receive a pass from teammates
        (i.e., forward toward the goal)

Name	Decision Making	Skill Execution	Support

Fig. 8.2 GPAI for invasion games. (Reprinted, by permission, from Griffin, Mitchell, and Oslin, 1997, p. 225.)

Mitchell and Oslin (1999) pointed out that the 1–5 scoring system is efficient for two reasons: First, observers who are primarily teachers do not have to record each time a player is involved in the game. In invasion games and some net/wall games, it is impossible to keep track of players' complete involvement because of the tempo, flow, and unpredictability of those games. This is especially so with players who have a wide range of skill levels. Second, the 1–5 scoring system makes consistency of scoring possible. Teachers need to create criteria for the 5 indicators (i.e., very effective performance to very weak performance), and the indicators should be based on lesson, unit, and curriculum objectives, as well as student abilities.

The tally system can be used with fielding (e.g., softball) and some net/wall games because they are played at a slower pace, which gives the observer an opportunity to tally every event. The tally scoring system provides an explicit game performance measure.

The GPAI can also provide students with a view of the bigger picture of their game play by calculating "game involvement" and "game performance." Game involvement can be measured by adding together all responses that indicate involvement in the game, including inappropriate decisions made and inefficient skill execution (see Griffin et al., 1997). One should not, however, include inappropriate guard/mark, support, adjust, and cover because an inappropriate response in these components indicates that players were not involved in the game. Game performance is a more precise measure and is calculated by adding scores from all components assessed and dividing by the number of components assessed.

Both teachers and students who have used a version of the GPAI in live settings to assess game performance have been considered reliable. In other words they have been consistent with a fellow observer in their assessment of performance approximately 80% of the time (Oslin et al., 1998; Griffin, Dodds, & James, 1999). The key to establishing reliability is in the quality of the criteria slated for observation. The criteria should be specific and observable (Mitchell & Oslin, 1999).

PEDAGOGICAL IMPLICATIONS

Because assessment should be an integral part of the teaching-learning process, there are certain considerations and implications that should be addressed to help teachers systematically implement the proposed instruments into sport-related games instruction. Both instruments provide information that can help guide teachers toward effective sport-related games instruction. Pedagogical implications focus on two primary considerations: (a) the process for yearly unit and lesson planning and (b) the construction of knowledge and skills.

First, teachers need to consider the notion of planning and in particular the notions of alignment between learning outcomes, teaching strategies, and assessment (Cohen, 1987). Teachers need to understand that planning what to teach is the same as planning what to assess and that there should be a strong link between these two facets of the teaching-learning process. The TSAP and GPAI can help teachers organize a *planning cycle* within and across lessons to help make the teaching-learning process more congruent. This cycle has three phases:

- First, students are confronted with a situation or problem to solve
- Second, students are in action (i.e., practice or game); and
- Third and last, students reflect on their action (i.e., critical thinking and problem solving).

For example, in a soccer lesson, students are asked to solve the tactical problem of creating space during an attack. Students are placed in an initial game with the goal of solving the tactical problem. After the initial game, students are asked to reflect through questions about their success in reaching the goal. Students are then placed in a situated practice that helps them practice creating space during an attack. Finally, students play another game similar to the initial game to modify and improve their game performance. Using a version of the TSAP or the GPAI can help teachers and students reflect about students' abilities related to an isolated objective such as the one described above or toward a more global performance that essentially reflects the sequence of a series of game objectives.

The second pedagogical implication builds upon the first and involves the construction of knowledge and skills. Constructivism is a theory about learning that describes learning as a building process by active learners interacting with their physical and social environment (Fosnot, 1996). A principle derived from constructivism that can and should guide games instruction is *reflective thinking*. By using either instrument, students are given time to reflect on such aspects of game play as choice of motor skill, individual and team decisions, and team strengths, which help them make meaning and connections across their experiences (Gréhaigne & Godbout, 1995). As mentioned earlier, to get the most out of the teaching-learning process, these instruments must be used appropriately. To this end, participating teachers who have used either instrument cannot stress enough the importance of using appropriate variables reflecting pursued objectives instead of always using the integral form of the instrument (Griffin et al., 1997; Richard, Godbout, Tousignant, & Gréhaigne, 1999).

CONCLUSION

Assessment can and should be a part of everyday teaching. The information that different assessment strategies can give students and teachers is critical to the regulation of the teaching-learning process. As authentic assessment instruments, the TSAP and the GPAI offer teachers the opportunity to promote the construction of game knowledge and skills. Authentic assessment procedures can help teachers teach and students learn about how to make connections within and among games (both intra- and intertransfer). Students clearly articulate that playing a game is a meaningful activity to pursue in physical education. Why? Playing a game provides structure and outcomes that gives meaning to performance. Students want to play games well.

The TSAP and the GPAI provide students with the opportunity to reflect and learn, through formative assessment, about themselves as game players. Both instruments provide students with both means and ends that are interrelated. Through game performance assessment students will learn that not only does each small element have a value but that each element is also a part of a coherent whole. Authentic assessment instruments such as the TSAP and GPAI can help teachers plan developmentally sound game experiences that can lead to more sport-literate learners and can help students better appreciate the playing of games.

II

The Teaching-Learning Process in Team Sports

9

UNDERLYING THEORIES
IN THE TEACHING-LEARNING PROCESS
OF GAMES AND SPORTS

In the present chapter, the evolution of the teaching-learning process from a behaviorist approach to a constructivist approach will be presented. Technical versus tactical approaches to teaching games will also be discussed to show the evolution of frames of reference in the teaching of team sport-related games.

The observation of current practices in the teaching of games shows a series of highly structured lessons. The first part is dedicated to a warm-up with or without a ball. The second part is based on the teaching of techniques, and at the end of a sequence of learning activities, games are played to integrate learned skills. Bailey and Almond (1983) state that such an approach, which stresses the need for developing motor skills before getting involved in the game, puts more emphasis on physical capacities than on the understanding of the game. Before them, Hughes (1980) indicated that understanding requires knowledge and perceptions. Despite the importance of decision-making and knowledge in effective game participation, there appears to be, at least from a constructivist perspective, little research in the area of student decision-making during game play either in physical education lessons or in organized sport. Researchers need to find ways of describing cognitive processes as they occur during a match. As a result, they would better understand those mechanisms that influence the interplay of knowledge acquisition and skillful performances.

The cognitivist perspective is intended for teachers who want to place their students in the center of the teaching-learning process and is based on a constructivist learning perspective (Piaget, 1967). Constructivism recognizes that awareness, although at first focused on the results of activity, must reach the inner mechanisms of such activities if true learning is to occur. This transformation of the learner in team sports takes place when the player meets and solves problems related to the configuration of the game in school and to motor performances. The player "constructs" their knowledge from a strong subject–environment interaction. This game-centered perspective leads to a "learner" rather than a content-based teaching style.

A CONCEPTION OF APPRENTICESHIP

Pedagogically speaking one uses the opposition relationship as a basis for all progress in the teaching of team sports in school physical education and sport settings.

Teaching-Learning Settings

One solicits students' affective and cognitive processes to foster an understanding of the principle of play and the mechanisms of game play. Tactical decisions and decision-making are favored for the construction of the player's capacities to anticipate the evolution of play configurations. The playful aspect also constitutes an important dimension. Indeed, one of the main functions of games in childhood is to develop a child's sense of identity and self-accomplishment. Nevertheless, a primary objective for a teacher is to create an instructional setting that will include a rapport of strength within a problem-solving environment.

To better understand the use of games at school, Figure 9.1 presents principles to analyze different approaches to games teaching.

This model is organized on two intersecting axes: on the horizontal axis, from specific to general; on the vertical axis, from simple to complex. Each of the four quadrants has particular characteristics.

1. **Simple/Specific.** This 1st quadrant represents the classical approach, with lessons centered on the learning of motor skills. The teachers work with a technique focus in their game teaching and offer a skill progression based on a preexisting list of motor competencies.
2. **Simple/General.** The 2nd quadrant represents the use of traditional games or innovated games as a subset of team sports. Traditional games are used as application tasks for reinforcing the

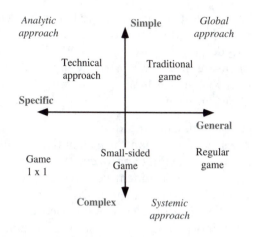

Fig. 9.1 A game analysis model (translation from Gréhaigne, 1994a).

subskills necessary to play a particular game: running with the ball, long and short passing, shooting, and so on.

3. **Specific/Complex.** The 3rd quadrant refers to the use of a small-sided game or modified game. Students are introduced to a mini game form close to the adult version of the game to preserve the meaning of game play.

4. **General/Complex.** The 4th quadrant refers to the utilization of the social-reference practice—the complete adult version of the game.

This diagram of principles for team sport analysis is not intended to put some normative value on teachers' practices. Rather, it makes it possible to establish a macroscopic assessment of a teacher's dominant conception. Depending upon class groups (age, motivation, number, coeducation, etc.), a teacher could use one approach or another.

As for other curriculum content in physical education, teaching practices for sport-related games may differ considerably depending upon one's views regarding the student's learning process. The ideas developed in this chapter are based on a cognitivist and constructivist perspective of learning. Also, at school, the learning of tactics and strategies in team sports is given priority over the learning of technical skills. This position is similar to the one put forward recently by many advocates of the Teaching Games for Understanding model (TGfU). Discussing what it means to teach for understanding, Good (1996) makes it clear that "teaching for student understanding" is associated with a constructivist view of the teaching/learning process. He writes:

"In the 1980s and 1990s, researchers have become interested in constructivist perspectives and in more detailed accounts of how students integrate and understand content" (p. 629). But, as mentioned by Cobb (1986), there are different constructivist perspectives. In general, one may identify two main teaching strategies while applying a teaching-for-understanding approach:

1. To propose to students the discovery of *the* tactical skill that applies in a specific situation. Such an option would be associated with an indirect teaching approach, combining both a subject matter–centered and a student-centered perspective. It could be referred to as an *empiricist constructivist* approach to teaching (Cobb, 1986), which considers that knowledge is an external reality and exists independently of the student's cognitive activity.

2. To propose to students the construction of suitable personal tactical skills that apply in a specific situation in which there may be more than one from the student's point of view. Such an option, also referred to as *indirect teaching*, would be associated with a radical constructivist approach (Cobb, 1986), which contends that the knowledge constructed by the student is the result of the interaction between his or her cognitive activity and reality (Gréhaigne & Godbout, 1995; Piaget, 1971, 1974a, 1974b).

The construction of sport skills by the students is therefore a process that requires:

1. That the students be presented with problems to solve or that they be put into situations favoring the recognition of such problems

2. That following the students' trials, they be presented with the result of their actions

3. That given these results, the students be invited to appreciate them and decide whether they are satisfactory

4. That following unsatisfactory results, the students be given the opportunity to experiment further and search for a better solution

Before going any further, it seems appropriate to summarize the postulates that underlie the view presented here concerning the construction of tactical knowledge.

1. **The learning process implies interaction.** The development and maturation of any individual take place through an adaptation to an environment perceived as a system of constraints and resources. At the outset, there is no formal object of learning defined as a

given set of solutions to be reproduced as is. The analysis of this adaptation necessarily includes the reciprocal action of a subject over the environment and of the environment over the subject.

2. **The learning process implies cognition.** Action regulation, particularly in the learning phase, occurs through mental activity whereby consciousness is but one aspect (Richard, 1990). Resort to conscious or nonconscious cognitive processes is essential for constructing knowledge. It is not sufficient for the teacher to state rules; the students must make them theirs. In a learning activity, the learners develop a self-regulation activity that consists of comparing the goal aimed for with the obtained result and analyzing the reasons for failure or success. This comparison allows an evolution of the ability to plan the selection of action and of the motor resources solicited.

3. **The learning process implies construction.** Faced with whatever situation, learners' knowledge, their ability to do certain things, and their development rest upon former learning. This development occurs through a new coordination of blocks of knowledge under the influence of internal or external constraints, forcing an adjustment of the learner's activity. In this sense, there is no novice at level 0.

4. **The learning process implies plasticity.** Plasticity represents a system's capacity for durably modifying its own structure and acquiring new skills. In the face of unusual situations, it is an organism's response capacity for developing new resources that will allow a better adaptation of the subject to the situation.

Given this frame of reference, we submit that *observation, critical thinking,* and *transformation* are three key elements to be considered in a constructivist perspective of the learning process in team sports.

AN OBSERVATIONAL APPROACH OF THE GAME PLAY

In the visual domain, to perceive implies decoding, putting different perceptions in order, and organizing information. In this sense, observation represents a critical moment in the teaching-learning process. Indeed, it allows information retrieval for both the student and the teacher. It provides for a simplified model of reality, but at the same time, it reveals which clues the observer gives priority to over reality.

One of the basic assumptions of qualitative research states that people develop various constructions of reality (Andreewsky, 1991; Bouthier, 1989; Gréhaigne, 1997; Gréhaigne & Godbout, 1995). We believe that the same phenomenon prevails in a classroom when many students and a teacher observe any given moment of the teaching-learning process. In such situations, observation may be looked at as a dynamic process involving the teacher, the student(s), and the action (the unfolding of the learning setup). This is shown in Figure 9.2. In the teaching and learning of team sports, we will more specifically refer to action as *game play.*

From a pedagogical point of view, one may view the observational situation from different perspectives. For instance, Figure 9.2 illustrates what might be considered a teacher-centered observational approach.

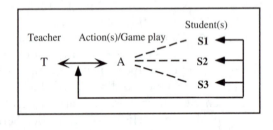

Fig. 9.2 A teacher-centered observational approach.

In this kind of approach, the teacher observes the action involving various students and then, on the basis of his or her frame of reference, provides feedbacks to the students, describing, explaining, justifying, recommending, and prescribing. What the students have perceived is thus confirmed if it fits the teacher's discourse or is put aside if it differs. In a learner-based teaching style such as that of constructivism, we perceive that the observational situation should be illustrated as shown in Figure 9.3.

While involved in the action or after its completion, each student is asked to collect or recollect information based on personal observations. Eventually, additional information may be provided by the teacher or by other student observers. We stress the word *additional* because the prime observer should be the player involved in the action. This is all the more critical because each observer reads action according to a personal frame of reference. Thus it is doubtful that an outside observer could duplicate the performer's perception of action. One could argue that in many instances an outside observer stands a better chance to perceive a picture closer to reality. Whether this is true or not

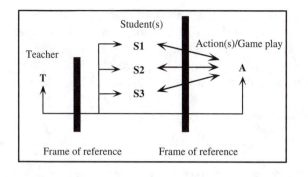

Fig. 9.3 A learner-based observational approach.

is, to a certain point, irrelevant. As stated earlier, the learning process, from a constructivist perspective, implies interaction between the subject and the environment. Augmented feedback is presented as additional information that can be processed differently by the learner depending upon his or her perception of the completed action and upon the learning stage exploited by the teacher (exploration, construction, consolidation).

If one argues that the learner cannot be replaced but can only be supported and complemented in his/her observational process, this does not imply that the learner possesses an innate and final observational frame of reference. As skill learning goes, so does observation learning. Therefore, the learner is also confronted with the construction of a frame of reference with the help of the teacher and other students. However, different decisions may be taken by the learner depending upon what the observations are focused on. Consequently, although constructed by each learner, the frame of reference must reflect the objectives pursued in the classroom. In team sports, we submit that the observation of game play encompasses four basic interacting elements. At an abstract level, one might say that they concern the static, dynamic, individual, and collective aspects of the game. At a more operational level, we shall identify them as location, movement, player, and configuration of play.

Figure 9.4 illustrates how one could perceive the observational situation and the ensuing communications in such an arrangement. At the center of the figure, one can see the action setting, involving a given number of students (e.g., 3 vs. 3; 5 vs. 5) in interaction with the subject matter; this interaction should eventually include reflection *in* action. Representing the observation setting, we have the teacher and student observer(s) observing the action setting, each one on the basis of a personal (maybe partly shared) frame of reference. A thicker line at the bottom indicates that the teacher also observes how each student observer proceeds, providing help if necessary. Finally, the various lines connecting members of a team (S1, S2, S3) and the team with the teacher and the student observer(s) illustrates the debate-of-ideas setting, involving reflection *on* action.

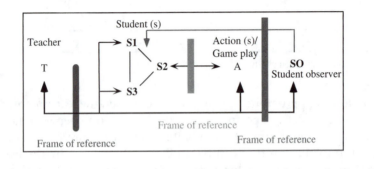

Fig. 9.4 Observational setting for the teaching and learning of team sports.

Finally, we wish to stress the fact that problem-solving learning and the construction of personal knowledge require reflection on the part of the students. Without it, the learner can only stumble blindly from one trial to another, hoping for random success, or wait for an outside observer to tell him or her what to do next. There is no understanding in either case. While verbalization may facilitate reflection, through informal (observation) and formal (TSAP; GPAI) observation will provide the basic data on which to reflect (Brechbuhl, Bronckart, & Joannisse, 1988). After many years of research and discussion in teacher education there is a common belief that important objectives of our teacher education programs is to develop *reflective practitioners* is an essential component of teacher preparation. If we follow the logic one step further, we should eventually come to the conclusion that a major objective of our school programs should be the development of *reflective learners.* Then, teaching for understanding will have taken on its full meaning, at least from a radical constructivist point of view (Cobb, 1986).

A SET OF SITUATIONS IN A LEARNING PROCESS

From a constructivist perspective, we perceive that the learning process in team sports may involve the successive use of three types of settings, shown in Figure 9.5.

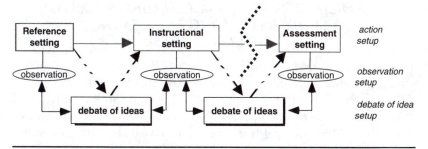

Fig. 9.5 Teaching and learning settings and setups (translation from Deriaz, Poussin, & Gréhaigne, 1998).

The settings are as follows:

- **Reference settings.** In which students are confronted with the actual practice of the sport or of some modification of that sport at the beginning of the learning sequence
- **Instructional settings.** Where students are asked to construct different tactical skills in response to problems brought about by play action
- **Assessment settings.** For providing students and teacher with information regarding progress achieved (i.e., summative and formative).

In connection with these settings and to facilitate learning, students may be involved in three different kinds of setups, as was illustrated in Figure 9.5:

- **Action setups.** In which students are engaged in the actual practice of a team sport
- **Observation setups.** In which students not engaged in the action setup are asked to observe peers and to collect information (usually with reference to performance criteria)
- **Debate-of-idea setups.** In which students are invited to exchange facts and ideas, based on observations collected or on personal activity experienced (Deriaz et al., 1998).

In all three types of setups, the teacher should keep in mind the importance of eliciting critical thinking. Teachers and students need to understand that the action steps during physical education lessons are designed for learning and constitute an authentic learning activity.

THE DEBATE OF IDEAS—A TEACHING STRATEGY FOR UNDERSTANDING AND LEARNING IN TEAM SPORTS

In recent years, several authors have discussed the development or use of critical thinking in physical education (McBride, 1991; Schwager & Labate, 1993; Tishman & Perkins, 1995). For some authors, the use of critical thinking is considered as an end in itself (McBride, 1991; Tishman & Perkins, 1995). Critical thinking is viewed as a learning objective, and the purpose is to improve thinking abilities, as illustrated by statements such as:

1. "Critical thinking is not and should not be limited solely to motor skill acquisition. The physical education environment is rich in opportunities for critical thinking" (McBride, 1991, p. 121).
2. "The nature of physical education offers a concrete context for exploring the payoffs of critical thinking that other subjects often lack: one can apply a useful exercise strategy, a plan for the game, or a new maneuver for a play" (Tishman & Perkins, 1995, p. 29).

Others, like Schwager and Labate (1993), views critical thinking as a useful tool that can help physical education teachers achieve their goals.

There are many ways of defining critical thinking. Given the purpose of this presentation, we will go along with McBride (1991) who "cautiously posit that critical thinking in physical education be defined as reflective thinking that is used to make reasonable and defensible decisions about movement tasks or challenges" (p. 115). Considering Tishman and Perkins' (1995) operational definition of critical thinking, we might add that in this presentation it involves particularly causal and evaluative reasoning as well as planning and strategic thinking. These authors have stated that "effective physical performance involves reasoning, reflecting, strategizing, and planning, all parts of the critical thinking process" (p. 24). Critical thinking is central to a constructivist view of learning (Good, 1996), but how is it to be used in the learning and teaching of team sports?

Let us consider four broad strategies that may be used by teachers at various stages of learning:

1. **Letting students explore.** At an early stage, students are put in play contexts, chosen so that they should present the students with problems or difficulties. After some exposure to play, students may fail to perceive any problem, and the teacher may then

     let them pursue further exploration with or without modification of the play context.

2. **Asking open-ended questions.** Once students have perceived and possibly identified a problem, the teacher may bring them to debate among themselves or with him or her by asking open-ended questions that do not direct them toward specific and pre-determined answers.

3. **Taking part in the students' debate and asking specific questions.** After asking open-ended questions, the teacher must be vigilant in moderating the students' debate by discussing the ideas and issues presented by students and asking them more specific questions.

4. **Having students reutilize suitable solutions.** Once students have come up with solutions that satisfy selected performance criteria, the teacher may then have them practice these solutions to stabilize their use.

While this last strategy is more routine oriented, the first three strategies all solicit critical thinking one way or the other. Strategies 2 and 3 are significant in view of constructivism and teaching for understanding and even more so when applied to tactical learning in team sports. General discussions, debates within groups of students, and debriefings (Dassé, 1986; Plummer & Rougeau, 1997; Tsangaridou & Sidentop, 1995) can complement one another in enhancing critical thinking and learning. In the field of general education, Good and Brophy (1994) have profiled some characteristics of a social construction view of teaching and learning. Among several of these characteristics one finds:

> Knowledge [is seen] as developing interpretations constructed through discussion ...

> Teacher acts as discussion leader who poses questions, seeks clarifications, promotes dialogue, helps groups recognize areas of consensus and of continuing disagreement.

> Students strive to make sense of new input by relating it to their prior knowledge and by collaborating in dialogue with others to construct shared understandings ...

> Students collaborate by acting as a learning community that constructs shared understanding through sustained dialogue (Good, 1996, p. 639).

We might say that what is sought is both reflection in action and reflection on action.

Evidently, discussions and debates among students or between students and the teacher involve overt and shared verbalization. Caverni (1988) has discussed verbalization as an observable source of information about cognitive processes. Considering the moment of its occurrence with regard to task performance, he distinguishes three types of verbalization: prior verbalization, which is considering what will be or ought to be done; concurrent verbalization, which is considering what is being done; and consecutive verbalization, which is considering what has been done. But why involve verbalization? It appears that verbalization settings should provide information about obstacles encountered by students in their effort to solve the problem at hand; such information can be used by the teacher or can be shared among students while debating about proper ways to perform a task at hand. As stated by Schunk (1986), studies demonstrate that verbalization can improve children's learning of information, modeled actions, and strategies, as well as their efficiency at performing tasks. Collectively, these findings support the notion that verbalization is a key process that can help develop self-regulated learning among children (Schunk, 1986, p. 362).

Gréhaigne and Godbout (1998) have coined this type of debate in physical education the debate-of-ideas. They defined it as situations in which, following game play action, students exchange ideas, based on observation or on personal experience. The debate may concern aspects such as the results obtained during the game action situation, the process involved, the tactics applied, and so on. What are the components of thought activity that one can identify in analyzing students' debate-of-ideas? According to Ericsson (1996) we can identify the following components in a general way:

- Intents or intentions referred to a purpose or a future state of the game
- Cognitions underlying a special attention to particular aspects of the setting
- Planning representing moves or states of game play mentally explored
- Evaluations expressing similarities among different possibilities

For their part, Hoc and Leplat (1983) differentiate the following:

- Verbalization about execution, which is the expression about a purpose or a state; expression about an assumption or a questioning about a purpose or a state

- Verbalization about the procedures (the subject expressing his or her way of doing)
- Verbalizations about assessment and justification
- External verbalizations about the general state of the subject; redefinition of the tasks

Figure 9.6 presents the relationship among settings, observation, and debate-of-ideas setups. The target is to do an alternation during a program of instruction to progress from the reference setting to the instructional setting and finally to the assessment setting.

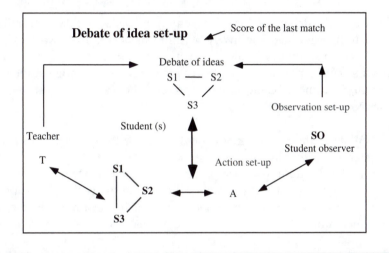

Fig. 9.6 The relationship between the debate-of-ideas and the instructional setting.

Depending upon the orientation of the debate, these debate-of-idea set-ups can be oriented toward different objectives, presenting some similarities with situations pertaining to the "setting theory" proposed by Brousseau (1986). Indeed, the debate-of-ideas may offer features similar to:

- Formulation settings, where knowledge plays a rational function
- Validation settings, where knowledge plays a solving function
- Generalization processes, where knowledge plays a reference function

Depending upon the level of conformity of students' responses regarding expected results, there is a change of plans to reduce the gap between the expected and the actual responses. One can consider, too, a stabilization of the responses, or an increase of the difficulty of the instructional setting to bring students to a higher level of performance.

Using verbalization in the teaching of team sports may help meet various needs, such as:

- Putting together a common frame of reference
- Acknowledging, conceptually, action rules (Gréhaigne, 1996) and management rules for the organization of the game
- Developing critical thinking skills that can be reinvested during the action in game settings

CRITICAL FEATURES OF THE DEBATE-OF-IDEAS

The use of the debate-of-ideas is an emerging pedagogical practice that needs to be examined attentively. Within this perspective, two axes are proposed to study this pedagogical strategy a little more deeply. The first axis concerns the choice of exchange modalities among students. The moment the debate-of-ideas is present, the teacher's and students' roles are of primary importance:

- What is the best moment for this debate to be beneficial in the teaching-learning process?
- Is the debate under the teacher's total control (Does the teacher ask all the questions and dictate the orientation of the discussion)?
- Is the debate interactive? Does the teacher assume the role of mediator?

The second axis corresponds to the types of questions to be asked in the debate:

- Are the questions open ended? Does the line of questioning pose certain problems that force students to refer to prior game responses?
- Does the line of questioning need to be closed until the desired response is discovered and given?
- Does the line of questioning need to be open ended until the desired response or responses emerge?

Teachers will adopt a way of proceeding based on the characteristics of their class-groups. In dealing with a difficult group, a teacher may be more concerned with keeping their classes busy and conflict-free and thus cannot foresee anything else in terms of learning. However, it is often easy to integrate a debate-of-ideas based on very practical notions. With other class-groups, it is easy to envision the debate-of-ideas in a variety of scenarios and different forms.

As stated by Janis and Feshbach (1953), communication often produces tension among students who do not use language very well. In the beginning stages of a debate-of-ideas, students expressing their thoughts often try to rupture the communication process. Their objective, although unconscious, is to escape the potential conflict of ideas that may arise by communicating in an aggressive manner (e.g., "Yeah, but Joey couldn't even hit the side of a barn by shooting like that.") or by trying to end the debate (e.g., "I don't understand nor do I care."). At the end of a learning process when students have been exposed to the debate-of-ideas, the discourse pertaining to learning evolves positively, notably due to the fact that students seem to engage themselves in the debate in a positive manner. Students center their attention on the theme of the debate and try to formulate arguments instead of trying to find ways of rupturing the debate or fleeing from it (Mahut, Nachon, Mahut, & Gréhaigne, 2000).

On occasion, it might be profitable to foresee a period of dialogue between student-observers and players instead of a debate-of-ideas. Discussions between students like "You lose too many balls" or "You are never available for a pass" can be very beneficial to a player's self-regulation in future game situations. Student observers often forget to tally certain game behaviors. Remarks on the player's behalf like "You forgot to indicate a shot on goal; I had 4 not 3" can lead students to a higher level of consciousness in relation to their game behaviors and responses. Hence, approaches like these, which solicit student engagement, are characterized by a process of guided discovery through a certain line of questioning (e.g., How can you move the ball effectively to maximize our chances of shooting on goal?) By exploiting dialogue, students are encouraged to analyze the problem or the obstacle to be surmounted and test out different solutions.

In conclusion, the time spent confronting ideas and reflecting on different solutions permits students to develop cognitive reflexes that bring them to higher levels of consciousness in relation to their performance. Deriaz and Poussin (2001) insist that these periods of confrontation and reflection should be an integral part throughout the whole learning process.

- In the **appropriation** and **exploration** phase, when students are presented with a game play problem and must find appropriate solutions that they already possess in their repertoire or build new solutions
- In the **validation** phase, when students are asked to show the pertinence of their solutions in action

- In the **integration** and **generalization** phase, when students are asked to exploit and integrate their learning in new game situations or more complex situations (Brousseau, 1998).

When faced with the production of a motor response, these attitudes must lead students to better plan game play behaviors and responses before and during play. The links between the indicators used for observation must be made obvious to students to be used for their reflection on their game play performance. The debate-of-ideas is founded upon verbal exchanges about game play to make decisions for future game play situations. We views it from a perspective where the appropriation of knowledge and the development of aptitudes are the main focus, with the goal of positively influencing practice based on sound reasoning and understanding. This perspective poses a problem: What is the connection between saying, doing, and understanding?

THE CONNECTION BETWEEN DOING
AND UNDERSTANDING

French & McPherson (1999) and McPherson (1993a) have stressed the importance of the verbal reporting technique as a tool to obtain information on thought processes of experts and novices when one wants to better understand how players perform. In our case, the purpose of the debate-of-ideas among students is to learn about action rules and decision-making through the use of verbalization in a social-cognitive-conflict setting. With respect to the doing/understanding duality, our work with physical education teachers has led us to distinguish four main stages of evolution in the learning of team sports. The teachers' awareness of such stages might help them plan learning sequences.

In a team sport lesson, at the *first learning stage*, students are able to take note of a result to analyze numerical indices and code what others do by analyzing, such as displacements and occupied spaces (Gréhaigne, Billard, & Laroche, 1999; Richard, Godbout, & Gréhaigne, 2000). In this learning stage the student codes the action of the performer which is a type of learning by doing experience.

A *second learning stage* consists, for the students, in describing their specific actions once the game is over. They get into a regulation process from one learning setup to another, provided that obstacles remain of the same kind. For instance, players will use long passes in European handball and basketball to outmaneuver a blocking defense located in front of the ball. Starting with questions from the teacher, players may also consider their former strategy or planning for this action in relation to the result of their action and thus construct an explanation for the results achieved (e.g., I succeeded because I did this or that). It is a learning stage that consists of *doing again* or repeating the action and following a series of trials, to use an explanatory description to begin extracting action rules.

In a *third learning stage* students can, while analyzing their actions, describe their peculiarities, provide reasons for their success, and generalize results obtained to eventually formulate action rules. Starting with questions from the teacher, players seek from their knowledge the available repertoire of answers and, from the results of their actions, the reasons for changes in their conduct. Hence, students are invited to formulate hypotheses about success requirements and to construct links between action and reflection on action. It is a learning stage that consists in *succeeding* and *understanding*, with the beginning of generalizations.

Finally, in a *fourth learning stage*, students can start questioning themselves on the basis of proposed learning situations, formulating hypotheses about the problem to be solved and about the way to respond. So, they are able to analyze the constraints of the task at hand and to determine specific related objectives. At the same time, they can formulate action rules and even associate them with principles of action. This self-questioning may lead to more complex or simpler planning. It is a learning stage that consists in *understanding* for *succeeding* and in *succeeding* for *understanding*, allowing student self-questioning whenever necessary *before* and *after* action (Piaget, 1974b; Wallon, 1941).

The four-stage model presented above is a hierarchical model but not necessarily a linear one. A learner may well move from stage 2 to stage 4 or move back to stage 3 when faced with too easy or too unbalanced an oppositional relationship. Nevertheless, concerning stage 4, one hopes that succeeding and understanding will be followed by a real improvement during the game and will not remain merely a discourse.

TECHNICAL/TACTICAL DEBATE

Research has been conducted on the technical/tactical debate, and little, for lack of sufficient time for experimentation and appropriate tools, has provided convincing conclusions on the tactical approach's superior influence on game performance (Turner & Martinek, 1992; Allison and Thorpe, 1997; Harrison, Preece, Blakemore, Richard, Wilkinson, & Felligham, 1999). The following section presents the results of an unpublished study in which the focus was to try to shed some light on the technical/tactical debate.

The Avallon Project

To control for a significant difference between both types of learning approaches on the development of students' game performance, an experiment was set up with sixth grade students (n = 24) chosen at random among all the sixth graders at Avallon school (France) assessment. Each of the 24 students was assigned to one of two heterogeneous groups based on results provided by using the TSAP (Gréhaigne, 1994; Gréhaigne and Godbout, 1995; Laroche and Gréhaigne, 1995; Richard et al., 2000) to assess performance in a modified basketball setting. The choice of basketball for this work corresponds to the desire to examine the effect of learning scenarios on students' decision-making skills in contexts where urgency is often called for. For this purpose, it was necessary to use a continuous invasion-type game rather than a game characterized by frequent starts and stops like volleyball, thus giving a period of time to plan the following game sequence. All the participants had had some physical education at elementary school, but very few had been significantly exposed to basketball.

Methodology

The Technical Approach The technical approach considers the technical requirements of the game of basketball as the central focus of what and how things are going to be taught. A typical lesson in this type of approach is made up of three phases: (1) a warm-up, (2) the learning of skills, and (3) a short game at the end the lesson. The main goal in these lessons is primarily the development of offensive skills. The skills taught during the 10-week experiment were the basics of ball handling, passing, receiving, and shooting.

The Tactical Approach In the tactical approach, the emphasis is put on tactical aspects of the game in relation to modified game situations (e.g., 3 vs.3, 4 vs.4). At the beginning of every lesson, the teacher sets up different learning situations, presenting a tactical problem to the students. In this approach, offensive aspects of the game are emphasized. The teacher guides the students in this process by helping them to get organized, read game configurations, and decide on appropriate responses. The teacher then helps students to regulate their learning.

Data Collection To assess students game play performance, the TSAP was used (Gréhaigne & Roche, 1993). Consequently, every student was estimated on the basis of:

$$\frac{\text{Attack Balls (AB)} + \text{Conquered Balls (BC)} = \text{Played Balls (PB)}.}{\text{Lost Balls (LB)}}$$

Through the different phases of experimentation, students were tested periodically, and a performance score was given to provide them with feedback on their adaptation to game play.

Organization of the Experimental Context After a few lessons of discovering basketball, the experimental part was conducted from weeks 3 to 13. Each group had 10 lessons of 75 minutes each. During weeks 9 and 15, a tournament was organized to assess students' evolution. During these tournaments, students were assessed using the TSAP performance indices. Players were assessed by 9th grade students who had observed at the beginning of the project for player classification purposes. All players were filmed during one match.

Results Of the 24 students, 9 improved their performance score between lesson 1 and lesson 6. Of these 9 students, 8 were from the tactical approach group, while only one was from the technical approach group. Eight students improved their performance score between lesson 6 and lesson 12. Of this group, 5 students were from the tactical group. Only 9 students improved their performance score between lesson 1 and lesson 12. Among these 9 students, 6 were from the tactical group. The results of the study are detailed in Table 9.1.

TABLE 9.1 Avallon Project: Game Performance Scores Throughout the Different Phases of Experimentation

	Lesson 1	Lesson 6	Lesson 12	Results 5 months later
Tactical approach group				
Mean performance score	11.48	12.74	13	12.22
Standard deviation	4.35	3.81	3.94	4.02
Technical approach group				
Mean performance score	11.35	11.33	10.90	10.28
Standard deviation	3.89	3.68	6.22	5.32
Average mean	11.41	12.03	11.94	11.25

As illustrated in Table 9.1, mean performance scores increased during the experimental phase, from 11.41 to 11.94. Many students progressed. However, it is of note that the highest mean appeared in lesson 6 (12.03). During the pretest in lesson 1, the mean for both groups was almost identical. At lesson 6 a rather important difference between the groups already appears in favor of the tactical approach group (1.41 difference between means). This difference was maintained itself through lesson 12, with the tactical group improving its performance level from 11.48 in lesson 1 to 12.99 in lesson 12. A slight but constant decrease was noticed in the technical group from lessons 1 to 12. However, game performance was again assessed 5 months later without any team sport instruction between the end of the project and this assessment period. The investigators in this project wanted to see whether any learning had been stabilized and was still present. Again all students were assessed with the same instrument used in the investigation, and it was noticed that both groups' performance level had diminished. Nevertheless, it was noticed that the tactical group had a lesser decline in performance due to the durability of learning created by the teaching context. When comparing means between the two groups, it was obvious that the tactical approach seems to have had a more lasting effect on performance over time (12.22 vs. 10.28) than the technical approach.

In light of this experiment, the tactical approach seems to create better results in terms of game performance if adequate time is spent. This approach provides students with a surer and more durable education pertaining to decision-making when faced with different tactical problems.

CONCLUSION

In this section we have presented the major theories that underlie the teaching and learning process of sport-related games. First, we examined the concept of apprenticeship in the learning setting (i.e., learning by observing and doing). We view the observation, critical thinking and transformation as key elements to implement a constructivist perspective to learning. Second, we presented the major ideas that underlie an observational approach to teaching and learning in game play. Third, we proposed a set of situations (i.e., reference, instructional, assessment) that comprises the learning process. Fourth, we present the notion of the *debate of ideas* which, we believe is a vital teaching strategy to help promote critical thinking in game performance. Finally, we examined the technical and tactical debate through the presentation of specific research.

10

CONSTRUCTING TEAM SPORT KNOWLEDGE

In chapter 10, we will examine the contribution of the Teaching Games for Understanding, explore the various contributions of the German and French of schools of thought to tactical approaches in games teaching, and present a new model for the teaching and learning of team sports. This new model will emphasize learning on the students' part, with their representations of the game, and teaching on the teacher's part, with the implementation of settings and strategies using observation, enhancing critical thinking, and thus allowing students to transform previous answers. The regulation of learning through formative assessment will also be discussed.

THE LEARNING PROCESS IN TEAM SPORTS: PRIOR AND CURRENT MODELS

In the evolution of team sport didactics, there were progressive changes between 1965 and 1985. In France, the Vichy congresses of 1964 and 1965 initiated an important change in the teaching of team sports (Amicale des Anciens Élèves de l'ENSEPS, 1966). At the time, three major problems were tackled from a new angle; these were (a) skill execution, (b) force ratio, and (c) changes to be considered in players' actions.

a. Skill execution would be considered as a perceptual-motor system in which perceptions play a major role.

b. The game, conceived as a force ratio, would be analyzed in a dynamic perspective to identify the structures at work with regard to team organization.

c. The player would be considered a member of a structured set, the team, which was organized in view of achieving some objective.

In line with these changes, learning consists of modifying the organization of the player's motor behavior based on his or her internalization of the structure of game play. Training loses its cumulative characteristic and, especially, leans on cognitive processes—perception and acknowledgment of signals—for internalizing structures. Subject matter is not *a priori* defined but rather is elaborated from a precise observation of the different games by the teacher.

With the emergence of structural analysis, the team is now considered different from the simple sum of the players who constitute it. The team becomes a structured set for achieving common aims (Teodorescu, 1965). There exists a reciprocal coordination between individual and collective actions. Our purpose is to show that team sports proceed from common tactical principles.

Mahlo's Model and the Tactical Approach

Mahlo (1974; originally published in German in 1969) studied game play phases and showed the complex character of "tactical action in play." He identified its components as follows (also illustrated in Figure 10.1):

- Perception and analysis of game play (resulting in knowledge of the evolution of the setting)

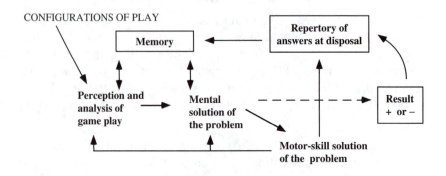

Fig. 10.1 The phases of game play according to Mahlo (1974).

- Mental solution to the problem (involving knowledge of the likely evolution of the setting and the representation of some plan of action)
- Motor skill solution to the problem (resulting in the practical solution)

The player determines distances, intervals, and speeds (hence, determining a subjective time to accomplish the task in accordance with his or her own motor skill). Mahlo put forward the notion of common referential and advance-organization in game play from perceptive aspects of the play. To gather information relative to this problem, he studied the answers of players and trainers from various levels of play who confronted different configurations-of-play pictures.

The modeling of practice presented in Deleplace's work (1966; 1979; 1995) gave birth to the school of *tactical approach* (Bouthier, 1984; Diaz, 1983; Reitchess, 1983; Stein, 1981); this school of thought postulates that "the intervention of cognitive processes is decisive for the advance organization and motor control of actions" (Bouthier, 1986). Its advocates hypothesize that this approach yields better results than two other pedagogical methods. One method, the *execution model* approach, focuses on the repetition, by the player, of efficient solutions produced by experts, while the other, the *self adaptive model* approach, postulates that judicious variations in the setting of the environment provide the most efficient means for the player to discover solutions and develop skills. The central strategy of the tactical approach calls (a) for the presentation of essential information concerning the tactical advance-organization of actions during game play and then (b) for the actual implementation of such actions in relatively self-sustaining and tactics-oriented patterns of play. These patterns of play, borrowed from actual game play, are not to be confused with traditional drills. They are selected on the basis that they can be played out independently of a match situation, that they call for tactical decisions, and that the outcome remains open-ended.

The Revisited Teaching Game for Understanding Model

In England in 1983, another model for teaching games, Teaching Game for Understanding (TGfU), was presented by Bunker and Thorpe (1983) and Kirk (1983). In relation to TGfU, the *Journal of Teaching in Physical Education*'s January 2002 issue presents two contributions concerning the evolution of the model. Holt, Strean, & Bengoechea (2002) note that in the debate concerning TGfU, the learner is at the center of the process, but the experience of the learner and his or her affective dimension have received only little attention within the English sport pedagogy literature. Pertaining to this topic, one can find contributions in the German or French literature (see Barth, 1994; Davisse & Louveau, 1991; etc.). Holt et al. stress that Thorpe et al. (1984) introduced four fundamental pedagogical principles aimed at developing physical education practices. These principles are sampling, modification-representation, modification-exaggeration, and tactical complexity. They are based on the concept of the transferability of key technical elements involved in games and the progression in apprenticeship. These four elements do not provide new information on the teaching-learning process in team sports. Research on transferability and linear progressiveness have provided very little evidence on the transfer of learning and the legitimacy of the use of progressions (in relation to skills and game situations) in the learning process. Using motor skills or knowledge in a new game or sport requires a certain reconstruction of skills and knowledge (Durand, 1989). Between transfer and reconstruction there is a gap that is characterized by the required time to learn.

After Bunker and Thorpe (1983) and Kirk (1983), Kirk and MacPhail (2002) present a new version of the TGfU model that draws on a situated learning perspective. This model is shown in Figure 10.2.

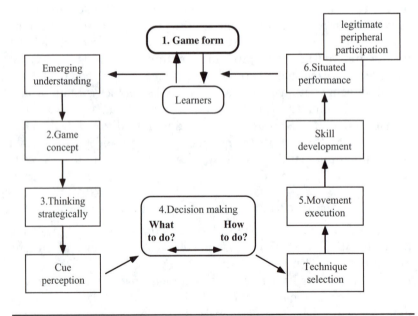

Fig. 10.2 The Bunker and Thorpe (1983) model revisited (Kirk and MacPhail, 2002).

A situated perspective assumes that learning involves the active engagement of individuals with their environment (Rovegno, 1999; Rovegno & Kirk, 1995). The notion of situated performance in the revised model provides one way of understanding the relationship between the game form and the players' representations.

However, these two new contributions to the TGfU body of knowledge fail to clarify the main problem with the TGfU model: What do students actually learn and understand from team sport instruction?

To better comprehend the reason for considering the "understanding" component in the TGfU model, let's briefly examine the relationship between theory and practice in physical education. Linking action to knowledge is a critical component of inquiry and reflective practice. In doing so, students do not apply theory in a learning setting but generate their own knowledge by questioning their practice based their own frame of reference. Thus, students have opportunities to connect practice to theory and theory to practice, enhancing their level of reflective thinking and broadening their scope of reflection in the pursuit of developing and improving motor competencies. The model resulting from this process brings us to conclude that in the learning process, approximate knowledge can help one make progress since it is because the model is approximate that it is likely to evolve. This being said, how are knowledge and motor competencies constructed by students?

The classical analysis model of the rapport between theory and practice proceeds from a *deductive logic*. Faced with a complex problem, it is tempting to adopt such logic, but there are limits to simplification. For instance, the simple learning of passing, dribbling, and shooting rarely produces an efficient performer.

A second model is based on an *inductive logic*. It is through practice, its meaning for the beginner, and the questions he or she is faced with that come first. Theory or knowledge is questioned following this practical phase. Within this perspective, practice and theory are intimately linked and interact constantly. The student's ability to extract knowledge from practice, relate this information to theoretical models, and return to practice constitutes the most certain way for avoiding a rigid theorization that would dictate game play.

The teaching strategies illustrated in this paragraph have been developed on the basis of theoretical choices and postulates about learning and on the basis of options about the function of the school. There is a strong link (filiation) between all of these prior and current models—the role of cognitive processes and tactical awareness. The part of understanding to anticipate on the following configurations is also crucial. In next section, we will present, in connection with the French tactical approach, a new model for the teaching and learning of invasion team sports

TACTICAL DECISION LEARNING MODEL (TDLM)

The use of the tactical approach (Rink, 1996) as framework, along with the contribution of a constructivist and cognitivist perspective and the accomplished work on tactical knowledge in team sports, has led us, in the context of school physical education, to put forward the "Tactical Decision Learning Model" (TDLM) (Gréhaigne & Godbout, 1995; Gréhaigne, Godbout, & Bouthier, 1999; Gréhaigne, Godbout, & Bouthier, 2001). This model focuses on the students' exploration of the various possibilities of game play and on the construction of adequate responses in small-sided games.

Figure 10.3 illustrates an operational teaching model that should enhance students' construction of tactical knowledge and the development of their decision-making skills. At the very onset of the learning sequence, students are put in action in some form of adaptation of the

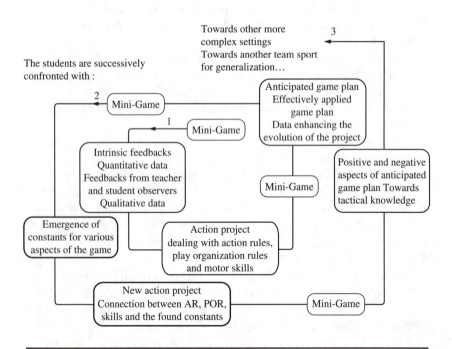

Fig. 10.3 A model for students' construction of knowledge in team sports.

game. For instance, fewer players should simplify the configuration of play. The use of smaller play areas however calls for some caution and should be balanced against the number of players involved since this may cause an increase in the time constraints, which are a limiting factor for decision-making (Gréhaigne & Godbout, 1998).

After appropriate observation, augmented feedback of a different nature can complement the intrinsic feedback experienced by each player. In the ensuing debate-of-ideas, each team puts together a first action project, which is then tried out in play. Following observation, the team's capacity for implementing the game plan or action project can be assessed and there may be proposals for an evolution of the plan. After a new exposure to play, students may perceive the emergence of constants for various aspects of the game. This in turn can lead to the development of a new action project with the introduction of connections between action rules, play organization rules (Gréhaigne & Godbout, 1995), and required skills on the one hand, and the constants that have just been identified on the other. After testing the new action project, the team may use the results of observations to appreciate positive and negative aspects of their anticipated game plan. In doing so, players are progressively putting together tactical knowledge and refining their decision-making skills. Once stabilization appears to be taking place, learning settings may be complex and, eventually, players may be exposed to another team sport to initiate a generalization process.

As one can see from this tactical-decision learning model, evolving from a first exposure to the pedagogical content to a state of stabilized knowledge of that content requires time. Thus, for students to truly construct new knowledge (i.e., knowing and doing) teachers need to provide more time and more progressions in their units.

MAKING SENSE OF LEARNING

For students to achieve and have success in relation to team games and sports, it is necessary to take into account the usefulness and appropriateness of the knowledge and competencies that need to be developed so that students can make sense out of the learning activities that are presented to them. Trying to make sense of a task implies that a learner will refer to his or her implicit or explicit formulation of the task, observable behavior, and cues before actually engaging in the task. How can we characterize the sense that students attribute to learning scenarios in physical education and sport? This notion can be defined as a particular evocation of the situation by the student, which is partially connected to his or her sociocultural background, by being in touch with his or her conceptions and representations of the content being taught, and by his or her intrinsic motivation. Furthermore, students' affective and intellectual resources must be taken into consideration to present learning tasks that have significance to them and that are accessible to them from a cognitive perspective. Hence, when presenting students to a new learning situation, a first step is to be aware of students' personal reference models to the task or activity being presented to develop adequate tasks.

A reference model can vary from student to student based on previous exposure to the activity. At the interface of a student's logic, the group's logic, and the logic of the game, a *reference model* establishes the conceptions conveyed by students. From this point of view, it is necessary to find a common ground between the teacher and the students with regard to the learning outcomes related to team sports and games. Is it not a simple question of making passes and scoring more goals than the opponents? The answers to these questions depend on the efficiency of learning.

There are three main categories of motivation:

- Play is perceived to be of relational interest: Students want to have fun; they want to be affiliated with a group. The end result or learning is of little interest.
- Play is an occasion for students to measure and prove themselves. Students are motivated on the basis of competition for social comparison purposes.
- Play is motivated by students' desire for improvement in the acquisition of knowledge and skills.

Often students analyze activities and distinguish among them the possibilities to satisfy that the activities offer them to satisfy the purposes for which they play. There are always students who have nothing to learn from the teacher or those who do not especially want to learn. All eventually agree very fast by refusing to actively engage in the learning activities. Nonetheless, students are in school to learn and thus progress and the conquest of "making sense" of what is being learned should generate interest and consequently pleasure.

TOWARD THE MODELING OF STUDENTS' PLAY IN TEAM SPORTS IN SECONDARY SCHOOL

In the present section, observation of practice and typical problems that students must solve to make progress will be discussed. The description of students' typical conduct makes it possible to model three characteristic stages for the "construction" of the confrontation by the students (Gréhaigne, Billard, & Laroche, 1999). With regard to the attack, these three stages are the *over-ball play*, the *relay play*, and the *forward-ball play*. Defense focuses on the *ball carriers*, the *potential ball receivers*, and the *stabilized space*.

First Stage

The first step is often observed in high school students whenever they have understood what is at stake in team sports: Their movements are oriented on the playing surface, and their actions lead them closer to the target under attack.

Organization Mode Selected descriptions of students' conduct deal only with successful setups that is, those that lead to a shot on goal. We think it more constructive to take into account positive aspects of success instead of analyzing hypothetical reasons for failure. In a match where both teams offer a comparable level of play, one often sees the setting of a first type of organization that focuses on two players. One player stays at the rear of the covered play-space (CP-S), playing the role of a distributor, and a second player plays at the front of the CP-S, attempting to score goals. Successful setups operate as follows: The rear player sends forward a long pass, over the group of players, toward the teammate occupying the role of scorer. The potential scorer takes control of the ball, gets as close as possible to the goal, and shoots; in doing so, he is hindered little by the players who eventually go after or accompany him.

In over-ball play, the ball is kicked forward, beyond the covered play-space, on behalf of a player who has broken away. Such a configuration of play favors a shot on goal. The distributor uses the long ball. The scorer has "constructed" (mastered) the catching-dribbling and dribbling-shooting coordination skills in movement and in game situations.

Evolution of the Pattern One can also observe for a given player the use of dribbling at the periphery of the play-space to make a pass or to shoot on goal. This type of organization appears when, for motor reasons, a player encounters technical difficulties performing the long ball pass. This is often the case in soccer.

At this stage, one observes numerous losses of the ball, but these organizational modes are always displayed every time an attack is successful with at least one shot on goal.

By the end of the first stage, a voluntary hindrance on the ball distributor forces players to adapt, and one begins to observe the use of relays. The teacher should make use of this new behavior because it foretells the functioning modes of the second stage.

Second Stage

The typical behaviors described in stage 1 being stabilized, the noticeable and lasting decrease in ball losses becomes a reliable indication of an evolution of the play. Still, without a real or apparent change in the number of played balls, one may observe, at times, a significant increase of lost balls. Does this indicate a sudden behavioral or learning regression? It is preferable to focus on the nature of the observed relations between attack and defense. These states of balance are changing, moving from the over-ball play to the use of a relay player.

Organization Mode The ball carrier is now subjected to a more efficient marking as soon as he or she gets possession of the ball, and the efficiency of the rear-distributor/forward-scorer system decreases significantly. The distributor-player's advance is hindered, or even impeded. The player often finds him or herself incapable of making a long pass forward. The player must construct a new solution for the problem he or she is faced with. The use of a proximate teammate, playing the role of relay, allows the ball carrier to get rid of the opponent and to find him or herself again in a situation close to that of stage 1. A player can then perform a long pass or advance alone toward the opponent's goal. But soon enough, the defense puts together an anticipation strategy on relays and potential ball receivers. Little by little, one observes a more rational occupation of the playing surface. This considerably slows down the progression of the ball and facilitates its recovery.

When observing the situation mentioned previously (the appearance of the relay player), one can quite often see two or three players taking charge of the progression of the ball toward the attack zone through a series of exchanges. This way of progressing toward the target offers the advantage of increasing both players' mobility and the speed of ball exchanges. This results in a significant increase of the covered play-space, particularly in relation to the width of the playing surface. For their part, given their placement between the ball carrier and the target, defenders display a deliberate will to recover the ball as soon as possible.

Interpretation Defenders' efficiency on the ball carriers greatly hinders their individual progression. Attackers must construct new solutions, most often by spreading themselves out or getting away from one another and from opponents. The play-space thus becomes noticeably enlarged (wider and longer), and one can observe a decrease in ball losses. Attackers have now mastered catching, kicking, and long accurate passes.

Following a first stage where focusing on the ball is paramount, the ball appears elusive, hard to control, and hard to pass along. Thus one observes, in the second stage, the appearance of a stronger focus on the opponent.

Third Stage

In stages 1 and 2, the attack–defense relationships are as follows: Attackers try to reach the target as fast as possible; defenders are anxious to display an increasing efficiency in hindering the potential ballholder in his or her efforts to recover the ball. What is then happening on the pitch when game play reaches the third stage?

Organization Mode Defenders settle and organize themselves in the scoring zone (or the offensive zone, from the attackers' point of view). This is a fundamental characteristic of stage 3; to make it simple, we shall call it *zone defense*. This setup forces the attacker to find a different scoring-action space. Progression of the ball may be like that encountered in previous stages, but the main difference is that the scorer no longer has free access to the scoring zone. She finds herself hindered by an organized and efficient defensive blocking. The attacker must therefore modify her usual way of doing thing: She resorts to relays. A new scoring zone, off the general axis of play, must be constructed between the attacked target and the defended target.

This defensive setup, intentionally organized in the scoring zone, results from the defenders' backing-off stopping maneuver observed in the previous stage (e.g., defenders floating so as not to be outflanked or run over). Defenders are positioned in a blockade between the target and potential receivers. They back off while facing the ball carrier. Once again, game play must be transformed since backing off is no longer possible once the ball carrier gets close to the target. It is no longer a matter of slowing down the ball carrier's progression; she must be stopped within the statutory limits, and above all, any scoring action must be countered.

The previous stage is both preliminary and yet essential for putting together a stabilized defense. Indeed, the defender's new task is all the more simple if he has been efficient during the previous stage, where his motor competencies underlie the results of his actions.

Later Evolution Faced with a new problem to be solved, attackers are forced to switch from a fast and linear offensive progression to a different management of their conduct, shown in Figure 10.4. They must rely on a variety of runs and also on the speed of exchanges to neutralize defenders. The objective is then to free a shooter in the scoring zone by providing her with a time advance on defensive repositioning.

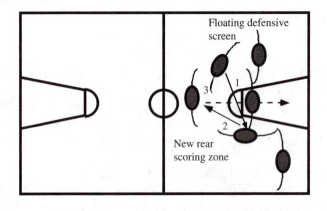

Fig. 10.4 Typical configuration of play for the new attack setup.

The new pattern for circulation of the ball is a convenient reference for an observer: From an almost exclusive circulation from the rear toward the front, one now witnesses a circulation ahead, laterally, and also from the front to the rear. This transformation results from the defensive setup, which, anticipating the generation of likely new scoring zones, comes between the attackers and the goal to defend the goal. On the attackers' side, game play typically displays a triangular circulation of the ball; this appears very rapidly in basketball and soccer. Its appearance in handball depends upon the players' construction of motor competencies that will allow them to perform long shots and over-the-defense (jump) shots with some chance of success.

In summary, the evolution of collective conduct always results from an interactive and adaptive solicitation on the part of the opponents (Bouthier & Durey, 1994; Gréhaigne, Bouthier, & David, 1997). Playing team sports is learning to manage positions and varying ball movements and trajectories. It is also learning to construct a rapport of strength with other players in conditions of decisional urgency in view of bringing the ball into the scoring zone and effectively scoring. Success requires the recognition or the generation of appropriate configurations of play that will make it possible to unbalance the opponents' setup.

These theoretical models of play are intended to help teachers better analyze what happens during team sports encounters. They are based on the theory of the construction of the players' strategies in play and by the play, as long as players are truly confronted with their opponents' adaptive logic. This teaching approach through game play questions the team sport coaches' *a priori* descriptions that use these stages as set stages for developing teaching content. The team sport model that we put forward works as long as one rests on a constructivist approach in which the confrontation dynamics with partners and against opponents remains paramount. This implies that the teacher, rather then applying high-level play observations to school situations, focus on the student's personal activity, with his or particular resources and cognitive functioning, trying to solve problems brought about by game play. In this respect, taking into account the specific context of school play is a determining factor in the teacher's analysis of typical conduct performed by his or her students in a particular situation (Van der Maren, 1999). It is only in action and in confronting a new situation brought about by the action that the student will be able to interpret and plan his action. In doing so, he brings in a new situation for the opponent and forces him to counter with original adaptive conduct, which, in return, enriches the dynamics of play.

Another model to help the analysis of the passes between players is shown in Figure 10.5.

The analysis of the different areas that a teammate can occupy in relation to the ball carrier permits us to define various categories of ball exchanges based on:

- The topological rapport between the ball carrier and teammates
- The direction in which players solicit a pass
- The position of the ball carrier in relation to the opposing team's goal
- Definition of support: A player is supporting the attack when he or she is available and accessible in an area in front of or behind the ball carrier
- Definition of calling a pass: To solicit a pass by initiating a run.

In our view, three conditions must be met for an effective call:

- A teammate must be in the ball carrier's field of vision
- A teammate must be at an adequate distance for a pass (accessibility)
- A teammate must be open to receive a pass (availability)

In short, attacking players should have teammates to support them who are in a good position, at an angle to receive the ball, at an angle

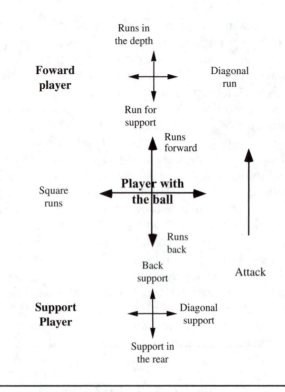

Fig. 10.5 A model to analyze ball exchanges among teammates.

that makes a forward pass possible, and at a distance that gives them time to make the pass.

In an attempt to characterize exploited game behavior at different performance levels, we can state that at a beginner level, the calling of a pass is often executed in inadequate or ruptured game conditions (e.g., calling pass in double coverage). At an intermediate level, the calling of a pass is often oriented forward or toward the opposing team's goal. Finally, at an advanced level, one can observe the exploitation of a variety of situations where players call for a pass. This exploitation will be based on the analysis of the rapport of strength in relation to the opposing team.

TRANSFORMATION

Students have truly learned if, when faced with a problem that is new but compatible with the resources at their disposal (inner resources), they have transformed their initial behavior and have identified and verbalized the action rules that made their success possible. "Action rules define conditions to be enforced and elements to be taken into account if one wants to insure efficient action" (Gréhaigne & Godbout, 1995, p. 496).

Transformation implies not only the appearance of new answers to a given problem but also a stabilization of such answers. Indeed the appearance of a new answer by the student does in no way mean that it will thereafter be used all the time. Under pressure, as in a time-constraint setting, a student may well reverse to a former and inadequate pattern of play. For new answers to be recognized as stabilized, they must meet three criteria: systematicity, durability, and generalization. *Systematicity* refers to a reduction in the range of the answers and a stability of performance over successive trials (i.e., the student will succeed 8 times out of 10). Durability means that after an interval of time without being exposed to the teaching and learning of a skill (for example, after a 2-month interval), the student can still perform at the same level. It should be clear that durability must not be mistaken for permanence. Durability ensures access to stabilized new knowledge until a new type of problem is encountered, calling for a solution pertaining to a higher level of performance or for a completely different type of solution. New answers must then be found, and the cycle starts all over. Finally, generalization refers to the student's recognition of a similarity between several situations and the subsequent utilization and reorganization of previously learned action rules; the reorganized rules are then applied in a given set or category of problems (Gréhaigne & Cadopi, 1990).

During game play, the teacher may conclude that new answers are being transformed into stabilized answers, therefore becoming a part of the student's resources in the following situations:

1. During game play, particular adaptations to the usual rules, like the use of a support player (i.e., joker) (Gréhaigne & Godbout, 1997), are no longer necessary and have been removed.
2. When confronted with a greater number of players during the game, for example, from 3 vs. 3 to 5 vs. 5, students keep using the same behavior developed during previous learning settings, such behavior indicating that newly acquired skills and action rules are getting stabilized.
3. When new teams are organized, players still resort to newly acquired behavior. This demonstrates that such behavior is part of the player's resources rather than associated with specific teammates and can therefore be called upon in play whenever necessary.

The construction and stabilization of new behaviors, then, rest upon the use of one or more of the following mechanisms:

1. **Sudden awareness.** It is an operation that brings to conscious level facts or events that were either usually managed by routines or had been previously processed by the student.
2. **Verbalization.** As mentioned earlier, it brings the student to describe orally what he or she has just done and, eventually, what he or she wants to do.
3. **Construction of automatism.** It consists in putting together motor or cognitive routines, most of the time through successive reiterations of the task.

To set these mechanisms on students, the teacher may have the students work on different types of tasks, such as:

- **Problem solving tasks.** They allow access to a superior level of understanding.
- **Nonautomated-performance tasks.** They correspond to situations for which general procedures are stocked in memory but must be adapted to the specific case at hand.
- **Automated-performance tasks.** They represent the performance of specific procedures, where reiteration remains the central feature.

During automated performance tasks, it should be noted that teaching for understanding does not exclude, at times, the construction of routines. These routines become "pre-established programs that put forward an automatic regulation in order to economically face relatively stable situations" (Gréhaigne & Godbout, 1995; 1997). Some of the problems brought about by a given configuration of play may then be managed rapidly as a background task without solicitation of the cognitive channel.

A routine is an internal operation used by a player that becomes automatic and is based on principles of economy and speed. When a routine is established, it works as a background application. The acquisition of cognitive routines not only results from repetition but can also be developed through adequate learning conditions. Several modes of acquiring routines have been identified by Leplat (1995) and Barbier (1996).

Acquisition through action involves intentional learning for which goals and objectives are developed but without any indication or operational means to attain them; controlled acquisition is common in formal scholastic or professional settings where acquisition of learning is based on knowledge and guidance is provided to the learner; and acquisition through osmosis involves nonintentional learning acquired without any formal instruction.

The modes of acquisition are not independent of each other; rather they interact with each other. In physical activity and sport, different types of information can provide feedback to a learner, such as the number of played balls in a certain time frame. Computer programs and simulators offer different possibilities for the development of more complex cognitive routines by offering players problem-solving situations in which they can learn proper responses to specific game situations (Blomqvist, Luhtanen, Laako, & Keskinen, 2000).

Routines have limited validity, depending on the variety of conditions in which they are acquired. They become inadequate when situations change. This limitation is, however, a favorable condition in their acquisition because these routines are simple and specific. What is important to know is what happens when a routine looses its validity due to unforeseen conditions. This failure, which interrupts a player's activity, forces a redefinition of the activity and thus a return to a conscious cognitive activity and to a state of lucidity. For example, experienced players have routines in their repertoire that allow them to consider other aspects of the game while executing specific tasks in game play. If a player is then confronted with an unforeseen situation, a different repertoire of possible solutions is put forth. The player's focus shifts to problem solving, which in turn permits the problem to be resolved.

When a routine is ingrained and becomes rigid, a player can continue his or her play. However, his or her responses are not valid to the game situation. The player does not obtain what was wanted, however, and his or her action, not taking into consideration the variations in the situation, leads to error. Moreover, the player does not necessarily perceive this error, as no other solution is available except the repetition of the same action. The player has automated the processing phase of possible cases and current incidents. For example, while attacking the opposing team's goal, the attacking team might be in advance on the defending team's repositioning, which represents an advantage in relation to time. A forward pass in an available lane, thus using the depth of the field, would help the attacking team take advantage of this situation. However, the player making a lateral pass to a partner will essentially lose the potential advantage created by his or her team's attack. Consequently, while the offensive team still has possession of the ball, the decision of using the width of the field instead of the depth in making a pass is not the best decision for the situation at hand.

When an exceptional situation arises, the player doesn't have the processes to find an original solution. Consequently, it can be affirmed that it is sometimes difficult to conserve the advantages of routines without loosing the advantages related to conscious mental processes. This game conflict is well illustrated using the notion of motor skills. Sport-specific skills have to be automated to meet game play requirements related to the speed of play. This automated process reduces the availability of more complex skills, which are needed to deal with and process different game play incidents (i.e., players who can adapt to the speed of play).

Nevertheless, it is true that competencies that are put forward to control a complex task suppose the acquisition of routines (Gréhaigne et al., 2001; Gréhaigne et al., 1999). These routines constitute the acquisition of higher-order cognitive competencies (Resnick, 1987). The situation has often been treated as the relation between skill and automated response. To this effect, Shiffrin and Dumais (1981) stated: "We think that automated response is a major component in the acquisition of a cognitive or motor skill, and we suggest that this factor be accorded a particular importance" (p.138).

Routines supply ready and available action units for higher-order activities. Routines and planned sequences define action blocks, which are used in regular game situations that have a foreseeable result.

In order to promote the players' construction of game competencies teachers and coaches need to create conditions and environments that consider factors that directly relate to the teaching-learning process. We will address some the critical factors in chapter 11.

11

CRITICAL ISSUES IN THE TEACHING
OF TEAM SPORTS

In chapter 11, our aim is to explore different factors that are critical to the teaching-learning process. In the first part of this chapter, our goal is to study in more detail team sports' and games' common traits without neglecting their distinctive and unique characters. Within this analysis, we do not want to distance ourselves from the regular social practices of sport but want to try and have a better understanding of these social practices to:

1. Try and maximize learning time in a school physical education setting
2. Avoid seeing students as perpetual beginners
3. Go beyond regular sporting practices that seem to hamper learning at the novice and intermediate stages by distorting the true learning objective, which is the development of game sense

COMMON TRAITS IN GAMES AND SPORTS
Transversality/Specificity

The notion of specificity relates to a linear evolution or progression in motor competencies ranging from simple to complex and from kindergarten to high school. In our view, however, we question this linear progression of motor competencies because of probable moments of stagnation due to students' biological and psychological evolution and the learning conditions that we present to students. Also, one can note that the evolution of action rules and motor competencies can be efficient and eventually be stabilized at a certain speed of play but can totally deteriorate as soon as the speed of play is increased. From an ideal learning perspective, the idea would be to be to integrate a few adapted similar and different action rules from a student's first exposure to team sport learning to the end of scholarship. However, the learning of action rule knowledge should be detached progressively from the objects from which this knowledge was originally constructed. The underlying hypothesis resides in the fact that action rules, grouped as guiding principles, can be reinvested in other games or sports with similar characteristics.

In relation to *transversality*, we put forward three postulates that we consider to be of importance in relation to the teaching-learning process of games.

1. Transversality is cognitive in nature. A student's development of knowledge and motor competencies is greatly influenced by a maturation process.
2. From the perspective of a specific learning outcome, transversality is relative to a specific classification of problems and must be understood as being in an indissociable dialectic with specificity.
3. Transversality must effectively be reinvested when a student is faced with a new learning situation. Transversality does not concern sensory motor skills, which are, in our perception, the necessary tools to put in place action rules.

Different action rules and principles of action have been presented in this book using these three postulates as guiding principles in the teaching-learning process. The presented action rules and principles of action can be exploited in different invasion games. Furthermore, it seems possible that, with certain modifications, they could be used in team sports of a noninvasive nature. We extended this conception to the construction of reference situations, learning situations, and success criteria that have common characteristics. In turn, this conception suggests that we should possibly limit the diversity of games when integrating children and adolescents into games to avoid disparity, thus having a focused vision on true and durable learning. This conception does not exclude the possibility that the specificity of different team sports can enrich a student's construction of new game responses. The end result of learning should be that students be able to consciously and more quickly construct more appropriate game responses.

Reproducing/Constructing

In the teaching-learning process, we make a strong distinction between reproducing solutions and constructing new answers. For the player, reproducing solutions involve the learning of a program of actions that is composed of a series of schemas of play. Theses schemas consist in preestablished sequences of action with singular technical skills, linked in a specific order and set in motion when certain specific game play events occur. On the contrary, constructing new responses implies, for the student, a capacity for using both determinism and random occurrences. The knowledge and motor skills constructed during action alter players' perceptions of information and their considered responses according to the lessons they draw from the events of the game. Progressively, players build up the capacity of quickly deciding, and this capacity itself rests upon the ability to conceive responses. In this case, cognitive processes serve to extract information from game play, to draw an adequate representation of the situation, to weigh contingencies, and to elaborate action scenarios. The resulting operative knowledge of configurations of play allows players to recognize restraints, regularities, and constants.

Theory and Practice: Toward a Practice–Theory–Practice Model

Educators have long been concerned with the separation between practical and theoretical aspects of teaching. Linking action to knowledge is a critical component of inquiry and reflective practice. In the case of physical education teachers, they do not apply theory in teaching settings but generate their own knowledge in questioning their practice based on a frame of reference. Thus, teachers have opportunities for connecting practice to theory and theory to practice, enhancing the level of reflective thinking and broadening the scope of reflection to multiple aspects of teaching.

The model that arises from this work allows one to assert that in didactics, approximate knowledge can help one to get ahead, and it is because the model is approximate that it is able to evolve. The classical analysis model of rapport between theory and practice adopts a top-down logic. Facing a complex problem, the temptation is often to adopt deductive and reductive logic; nevertheless, simplification has limits. For example, the learning of passing, dribbling, and shooting rarely produces an efficient performer.

A second model is based on a bottom-up logic. This model is based on the sense that a novice player makes out of the initial contact to different game play situations. Theories or scholarly knowledge are integrated into this practical process. In this perspective, practice and theory are intimately linked and function with constant interactions. Extracting knowledge from practice, confronting these data to theoretical models, and returning to the practice constitute the most certain means of avoiding a theorization that prescribes game play.

Reversibility/Stability

The notions of reversibility and stability are based on the idea that in a complex setting, there exist several solutions or attitudes that constitute an adapted response for a given situation. Several distinct situations also exist, where a same or similar solution or attitude can constitute an adapted response. For students, a good adaptation to a similar problem in different classes depends on a combination of different factors. Hierarchy and the importance of each solution can vary considerably for each player, with apparently similar results.

The state of equilibrium is precarious, and its main feature is reversibility. An experienced player, because of a temporary failure or stress, can reverse, for a moment, to behaviors associated with novices. The dispersion of the elements that constitute a behavior is more important in a complex setting than in simple tasks. This idea suggests that the organization of elementary processes in more complex procedures introduces variations particular to this organization. We are confronted with a system of variables whose interrelations can explain the variations or stabilities observed. Consequently, the expression "adaptable procedure" means that the random aspect of certain behaviors has been selected. This process makes it possible to constitute routines that offer the player the possibility to function with economic schema in many settings (Houdé, 1992). The schema present the possibility of being at the interface between awareness and automatic regulation.

ADAPTATION AND LEARNING IN RELATION TO TEAM GAMES AND SPORTS

The second part of this chapter proposes to focus on the learning of adaptability and decision-making rather than presenting ready made "recipes." In sports, there is always a need to adjust for the active opponent trying to interfere with one's skill execution. In soccer, rugby, or similar invasion games, where continuous play is ensured by the rules of the game, resorting to play schema is rarely appropriate since, as the game unfolds, disorder settles rapidly. Tactical knowledge, then, comes into play.

To facilitate the learning of such tactics, we propose a combination of two teaching procedures. The first way to bring about game situations requiring adaptation and decision-making is to use, in various ways within the same sport, a *joker* playing the role of a support player. By analogy with card games, we call the "joker" a player to which specific roles have been assigned, after due transformation of the usual rules of the game. Pedagogically, the use of a joker is very significant for two reasons: First, beyond the simple change of rules, the specific location and role assigned to the joker force a subtly oriented adaptation on the part of the students for them to solve a new problem requiring both a strategic and tactical solution. Second, depending upon the specific role assigned to the joker, the teacher may choose to select a good or a poor player to play that role. In cases where the joker's role does not require good motor skills, assigning a poor player will do a lot of good to the student's ego and give him or her a chance to improve passing skills as well as decision-making. It should be clear for the reader that the expressions "joker" and "support player" will be used interchangeably; in the classroom, however, teachers should systematically use the expression "support player" since it is the joker's function within the team.

The second teaching procedure, aiming at getting students to recognize the similarities among different sports in term of tactical skills, consists in moving, in a short time interval and sometimes during the same class period, from one sport to another to facilitate a reappropriation of the tactical skills in a different context (i.e., other required motor skills, different rules, etc.) and therefore avoid too close an association between given tactical skills and one given sport.

One may wonder why so much emphasis is put on the development of decision-making and adaptation skills. If what is learned in physical education is to have any carry over value, though, one must recognize that a life-long practice of team sport calls for continuous adjustment:

- To various levels of one's ability over the years
- To different levels of players
- Sometimes, to different sports

Using a Joker in Different Team Sports During P.E. Classes

To illustrate the teaching process and the learning strategies resulting from the use of the teaching procedures described above, we now present a series of four exercises involving three team sports: European handball, soccer, and basketball. As alluded earlier, one way of increasing the learning outcomes is to provide opportunities for the students to articulate several sports. The players can analyze how they play the game from one sport to the other and can discuss tactical choices among themselves.

For each exercise, the reader will first find the principal action rule to be used or to be acquired by the students. Action rules (Gréhaigne, 1989; Gréhaigne & Godbout, 1995) refer to conditions to be looked for and to the elements of the game to be taken into consideration if one wants to ensure efficient action. Tactical knowledge about team sports basically rests upon such rules; their use allows a player to solve problems encountered during the game. Focusing on action rules is a choice that clearly favors the understanding of the action. After having stated the principal action rule at work, we will provide details about the organization for practice, about specific instructions, and about points for the teacher to observe.

The reader will note that the intent of such exercises is to have the students experience the advantages and difficulties inherent to each specific condition of play and to progressively discover which condition appears more efficient; eventually, in the regular practice of the sport, the search for such a condition will allow the application of the action rule. As proposed here, the use of such exercises is intended for the students to discover which condition of play works better and which tactics or strategy ought to be favored when a problematic condition of play is encountered.

Exercise 1: European Handball

Action rule: To score, the team must bring the ball rapidly ahead of the effective play space (a play space is any area where a group of players are effectively engaged in the action).

Organization for Practice The practice takes place on a 40 m × 20 m European handball field. Inside this area, there are six players against six players, with each team consisting of a goalkeeper, four regular players, and a support player (the joker).

Specific Instructions To force the action ahead to the effective play space and in open space, the support player is placed inside the 6-meter area. The ball must be given to the joker before a goal can be scored. The support player cannot score, and the goalkeeper must stay on the goal line.

Points for the Teacher to Observe When a team regains possession, the ball should reach the support player as quickly as possible.

Observe the quality of the first pass because it will determine whether the team stays in advance of the opponents. The players moving into open spaces should plan their run so as to receive the ball in front of them.

Exercise 2: European Handball This is the same exercise as exercise 1, with the same action rule, but now the goalkeeper is allowed to move and defend in the 6-meter zone with the usual rules for defense in European handball. The teacher will observe especially the counterattack when a team regains possession. Then, when the students appear to have learned and used this first action rule (bringing the ball rapidly ahead of the effective play space), the teacher can introduce other action rules, such as:

- Reducing the time to bring the ball in the scoring zone
- Moving away from opponents
- Moving into available intervals (free space between opponents)
- Moving behind the opponents' backs
- Using speed and temporal advantages (temporal advance)

By doing so, the teacher initiates tactical learning on the players' parts. Students are not given recipes to apply but are invited to consider the problem brought about by the specific setting, to discuss it within the team, and to decide upon some solution, thus constructing a collective action project.

Exercise 3: Soccer Then, in a second part of the class period, the teacher continues to focus on the learning of efficient action rules. The players apply the first action rule mentioned above but in connection with a different sport.
Action rule: To score, the team must bring the ball rapidly ahead of the effective play space.

Organization for Practice Outdoors, the practice takes place on a 50 m × 30 m surface with 6 m × 2 m goals. Inside this area, there are five players against five players, each team consisting of a goalkeeper, three regular players, and a support player (joker). Indoors, the game can be played on a European handball court but without goalkeepers (four players against four players).

Specific Instructions The teacher places the joker within the 6-meter area. The ball must be given to the support player before a shot at goal. The joker cannot score. When a team regains possession, the ball should reach the support player as quickly as possible.

Points for the Teacher to Observe

1. The quality of the last pass should be noted because the strikers must have time to adjust their location to shoot. Any player moving into an open space should arrive at a "favorable receiving angle" (Hughes, 1980, p. 76) with respect to the defender by outrunning him or her or by falling back.
2. The pass should be directed behind the defender and in front of the attacker.
3. The direction of the ball passed by the joker should be to the better foot of the striker in a face-to-face fashion (that is, in line with the player's run).

The interactions between teammates and opponents are numerous, and the role of the support player is critical. This third exercise should lead to a beginning of generalization with a positive transfer.

Exercise 4: Basketball
Action rule: Playing the ball ahead.

Organization for Practice The practice takes place on a basketball court. There are four players against four players, each team being made up of three regular players and a support player.

Specific Instructions To obtain a play located ahead of the effective play space, the teacher places the support player in a small area at the top of the key. The other players are not allowed to enter that area. The ball must be given to the support player before points can be scored, except in the case of an offensive rebound. The joker is not allowed to score.

Points for the Teacher to Observe.

1. The quality of both the first and the last passes.
2. The students should be shooting while moving forward.

The Management of a Class for Optimal Learning

Beyond some obvious differences, like attitude and morphology, a class of students is made up of unique and original individuals.

Teachers have to manage the learning of such a class-group, in which, at each moment, interactions between the individuals can modify individual or group behavior. The management and proper functioning of a class-group supposes that certain particularities be taken into consideration.

In relation to the teaching of team games and sports, one the first encountered problems resides in the constitution of work groups or teams. Not everybody is interested or wants to actively participate in the content being presented. This can be the result of girls and boys being in the same class, bad experiences in previous physical education classes, and so on. In teaching team games and sports, the grouping of students into different teams presents contradictory requirements, between stability and adaptability. One thing remains certain: When grouping students, the result of a confrontation shouldn't be determined by the teams' composition. How can a teacher use the diversity of his or her students as a positive element instead of perceiving it to be an obstacle? What are the principles of forming work groups that will promote the learning process of team games and sports? How does a teacher manage a classgroup composed of boys and girls in a games education setting?

To answer these questions, different perspectives from the physical education literature in relation to the grouping of students are presented, and an analysis of the advantages and disadvantages is put forward. Finally, the qualities, weaknesses, and potentials of student groupings will be discussed in light of specific confrontational problems in games education.

Team Dynamics The notion of *team dynamics* is presented based on the contributions found in international literature on sport pedagogy.

Contributions from Anglo-Saxon Literature "Team work is the essence of life" (Riley, 1993, p. 15). One of the most gratifying and exciting experiences for a team sport player or coach is to be part of a team that has cohesion and is successful. However, building an efficient team takes time and effort to achieve success. It is always a paradox to see a talented team performing with mediocrity because they cannot exploit their resources adequately when less-talented teams perform better because of a greater cohesion within the group. If too much energy is focused on developing and maintaining a group's cohesion, this energy expenditure is often unavailable for constructing a team's game play performance. Teammates must interact, work together toward common goals, adapt to various demands, and equilibrate personal aspirations to group objectives. This particular theme has not been addressed extensively in the sport psychology literature. Hence, there is a need to improve our comprehension of a team's functioning to have a better grasp of what types of systematic interventions can be developed in the early stages of team building.

Although all teams are considered to be composed of a group, all groups cannot be considered teams (Parker, 1990). Generally speaking, a team represents a certain type of group. Carron (1988, p. 7) explains that teams, in a sport setting, are characterized by a collective identity, an acute sense of collective objectives, structured interaction procedures, structured methods of communication, and personal and collective independent tasks.

Teams are in constant evolution, changing to adapt to internal and external factors. These changes can be minor and not perceivable or major and necessitate significant modifications. Carron (1988) suggests that the development of a team can be described by linear, pendular, or cyclic models. When a team develops itself, it can take different courses in relation to these models.

All teams want to be efficient and perform well. Efficiency can have different meanings, depending on the composition of a certain team. It depends on the prescribed task, resources, and the state of development of the team in question. The prescribed task could be related to game rules. The available team resources rest upon the knowledge and motor competencies of each team member. The variable "resource" specifies the type and the cost of available resources, while the prescribed task defines the team's needs in terms of resources and how these resources should be used. A group's state of development consists of the existing interpersonal relationships among the group's members and their influence on the group's performance (Sherif & Sherif, 1979). In particular, Hanson and Lubin (1986) insist on the engagement of team leaders for a team to be successful.

This relatively linear and continuous perspective of team development is somewhat different from a dialectical perspective that is more predominant in certain European schools of thought. The next section will address some of the predominant French perspectives.

The French Tradition To better situate a discussion on team building from a French perspective, different elements from the literature will be presented in relation to complexity, required variety, and opposition rapport. Finally, the team as a social organization will be the object of a distinct presentation.

The Notion of "Team" in a Team Sport Setting The psychosocial approach to the investigation of team dynamics was inspired by Lewin and his collaborators in the 1950's. From this approach, numerous studies on team dynamics, and its various components (its genesis, cohesion, climate, communication networks, psychological preparation, leadership styles, etc.) have been accomplished. Based on the abundance of accomplished work, here are but a few examples of authors and their main research interests:

- Rioux and Chapuis (1967; 1976) studied team cohesion.
- Anzieu and Martin (1968); Carron (1986): studied team cohesion.
- Mérand (1977) studied team sports as an original modality to study group dynamics. The dynamics within a group where individuals oppose each other is often characterized by the complexity of problems or obstacles put forward to hinder the opposing team's performance while trying to resolve the problems put forward by the opposing team.
- Gréhaigne (1989) studied the force ratio between two teams in a teaching-learning context. The force ratio, as defined previously in this book, is the antagonistic links that exist between players of opposing teams, which are due, in part, to the application of certain rules of play that determine interaction between teams. The essential elements in this research topic have provided the foundation of future study of the teaching-learning process in team sports.

Modified Games: A Case of Presenting Minimal Complexity A common theme in much of the team sport literature is related to the *collective dimension*. In his definition of team sports, Gréhaigne (1992) mentions that the force ratio is characterized by two groups confronting each other. In light of creating a teaching-learning context that is adequate in the construction of tactical competencies, it is proposed that modified games should be 3 vs. 3, which Gréhaigne considers to be the minimal number of players for a game to be considered a team game. Below this number of players, modified game situations represent various incomplete configurations of play when considering the confrontational aspect of team sports. Constructing complexity in team sports involves much more than going from a 1 vs. 1 situation to a 2 vs. 2 situation and so on. Three vs. three situations allow a teacher to construct learning scenarios where students have to go beyond binary choices— keeping the ball or passing it to his or her partner—to preserve an important aspect in team sports, which is playing without the ball. The ball or projectile confers to its handler a particular status composed of responsibilities concerning tactical choices.

Group Stability: A Question of History and Permanence In trying to understand a team sport player's behavior, one must assess this player in relation to the rest of the members of the team. A player's game responses are often the product of a situation's characteristics and the constraints and opportunities as he or she sees them. Taking into consideration a player's responses as pertinent is to rediscover a game situation and the unforeseeable responses it can generate. This process can help analyze the player–game interaction. The analysis of this interaction, through observation, can aid in determining how members of a given team can structure their cooperation for both offensive and defensive purposes.

Bernard (1963) described a team as a totality under construction. Both time and history are important elements in the genesis and life span of a team. In relation to physical education, Plummer and Rougeau (1997) insist on the necessity of analyzing the repartition of status and tasks within a group while systematically reserving adequate time for a group's regulation.

SPORT ETHICS

From an ethical point of view, succeeding in team sports means that rules must be considered a key element for game play. They are essential for advancing, yet also ensure the security of students. We must conceive of refereeing as an indispensable help to the understanding of play mechanisms.

Efficiency is an unavoidable aspect of the game and plays a central role in team sports, as in any sport. Most of the time, the result of a match determines winners and losers. Team sports must nevertheless remain a courteous and codified assault in which the presence of a referee, through its regulative function, reduces considerably the hazardous nature of a warlike confrontation. The very notion of "courteous assault" may force a smile. But in this case, an important aspect concerns the distinction between competition and emulation. The competition can introduce hostile relationships with other players when opponents are perceived as people to be dominated. Emulation represents a means to compare oneself to another player and to exchange with that player in considering who he or she is. Emulation is a source for success because it allows a comparative approach with the other to discover the similarities, the differences, and the progress one has made. Also, in educational contexts, the search for fair conditions of play, such as reasonably balanced teams, should constitute a background on which to select the learning objectives and the teaching procedures. Looking for the most efficient strategies and tactics should not lead to a victory-at-all-cost attitude because for the school it becomes a Pyrrhic victory. In this sense, the rightful place of ethics in the teaching of team sports and games needs to be considered.

The content in the first 11 chapters of this book has focused on the underlying theories that support a constructivist learning perspective in team sports and games. Our beliefs, knowledge and convictions regarding the teaching-learning process of sport-related games bring us to the presentation of the Tactical Decision Learning Model (TDLM). The TDLM promotes a student-centered model to games learning. In the present chapter we present factors to help you maximize the implementation and effect of the TDLM. Chapter 12 will focus on various aspects of research that need to be considered in order to continue our collective work relative toward building a better games theory for sport-related games teaching and learning.

12

RESEARCH AND DEVELOPMENT: WORKING TOWARD EVIDENCE-BASED PRACTICE

There is a gap between research on teaching and learning sport and teacher and coach practices and development. This gap between the institutional and scientific discourse and professional practices shows how difficult it is for knowledge to penetrate into the fields and courts where physical activity is taught. What are the specific and essential game knowledge structures that ought to be taught? How do teachers and coaches adapt the content in light of the development of efficient tactical and motor skills and movements in their students? On which precise basis is a given progression proposed, and more specifically, are the articulated levels determined by teachers? These types of questions go beyond the classical thoughts about the relationship between social practice and school practice.

Thus far we have examined the teaching of team sports in the light of a new team-sport didactic approach at school with a constructivist and cognitive approach. We have provided an overview of historical aspects concerning conceptions of teaching in team sports, and presented the *Tactical-Decision Learning Model* (TDLM) with reference to French and German literature. We also have provided you with a model of players' activity using invasion games. We have argued that the TDLM, the modeling of the practice, the team sport assessment procedure, and the observation tools discussed in this book appear to produce an objective, reliable, and valid indication for interpreting the player activity.

The purpose of this chapter is twofold. First we will argue for research and development work (i.e., data-based not data-free development) that should be pursued to develop the knowledge on a team sport learning-teaching system. From a novice status to that of an experienced player, there is a qualitative transformation. Rather than resting on incidental learning, we should seriously study this transformation process and strive to better understand how learners construct their competencies and their motor skills to make appropriate action during play. Second, we will present two theoretical frameworks that hold strong possibilities for more closely examining the strength of the TDLM. To accomplish this we need to consider the following:

1. We (i.e., teachers, coaches, teacher educators, and researchers) need to value field-based research. Field-based research, while messy and trying at times, needs to be an essential part of good development work, thus leading us toward evidence-based practice.

2. We should consider more programmatic research (that is, a plan under which small steps can be taken). This might involve a couple of institutions following a particular theoretical framework, each carrying out a shared but separate research agenda. We are not advocating that we all take this on, but this type of research could lead to more robust findings.

3. We must ground our research questions in a theoretical framework that can help lead to strong research designs and thus more robust findings.

Similar to the Teaching Games for Understanding (TGfU) model, the TDLM is centered on getting students engaged in a game-like manner and thinking about the tactical problem on which instruction is focused and designed to develop tactical awareness (i.e., decision-making) (Griffin, Mitchell, & Oslin, 1997). As with all teaching methodology TGFU makes some assumptions about how students learn (Rink, 2001).

To further our understanding of the TDLM, it is important to employ multiple theoretical perspectives in the design and interpretation of sport-related games research. We advocate two theoretical frameworks for information-processing theory and situated learning theory to investigate how individuals learn and how prior knowledge of subject matter (i.e., games) that learners bring to instruction influences the teaching and learning process.

EXPLORING THE DEVELOPMENT OF LEARNERS' GAME KNOWLEDGE

As research on games teaching and learning evolves, and as the debate concerning technical-versus-tactical approaches to games instruction subsides, sport pedagogues must begin to move forward and explore new and important avenues of study. As Rink (2001) argued, "when you spend all of your effort proving that a particular kind of teaching is better than another kind of teaching, you limit what you can learn about the very complex teaching/learning process" (p. 123). Grounding work in learning theories that underlie different teaching methods and approaches to teaching will enable researchers, teachers, and curriculum experts to create a knowledge base that extends beyond identifying direct links between what a teacher does and what a student learns to begin to test the assumptions of different methodologies. For instance, in the case of TDLM, application of a theory of learning may enable researchers to ask questions that examine the assumptions the model. For example, does the constructivist nature of this model lend itself to more motivated learners? How do learners construct knowledge of games, strategies, tactics, and decision-making in games?

Sport pedagogy researchers have argued that instructional strategies should be based on learning theory because without a clear understanding of how students and teachers learn, one cannot expect to achieve intended learning outcomes (Kirk & MacPhail, 2002; Rink, 2001). Researchers with a learning orientation put an emphasis on understanding what students know, can do, and bring to sport-related games (prior knowledge) and how their knowledge changes as a function of games instruction (Griffin & Placek, 2001).

Information-processing theory from cognitive psychology provides a theoretical framework for investigating domain-specific knowledge and contributes to ideas of what learners know and how they learn cognitive aspects of movement activities. Information processing suggests that humans represent the world through knowledge structures stored in long-term, intermediate, and short-term memory (Shuell, 1986). These knowledge structures are formed by gathering and combining forms of new information and then by relating the newly acquired information to prior knowledge already stored as representations in long-term memory (Sternberg, 1984). These knowledge structures consist of nodes that represent particular concepts, facts, or theories and relate hierarchically to other nodes in an array of relationships (Anderson, 1976; Dodds, Griffin, & Placek, 2001).

Information-processing research reports that complex knowledge structures internally represent the outside world and can be changed under various conditions over time (Dodds et al., 2001). Further, knowledge can be broadly characterized as declarative, procedural, conditional, and strategic (Alexander & Judy, 1988; Anderson, 1976). Sport pedagogy research reveals that individuals may simultaneously be highly knowledgeable about some aspects of sport and physical education while far less knowledgeable about others. For example, individuals in a physical education setting in the same class in school will differ greatly in their knowledge structures of sport-related games. A student could be highly knowledgeable about the tactics involved in invasion games while their knowledge structures relating to the tactics of net/wall games may contain many gaps.

From a perspective related more directly to instruction, Gréhaigne and colleagues' theoretical papers have explored players' acquisition and use of knowledge, expanding our views of how to teach strategic and tactical knowledge in the context of game play. Drawing on the motor learning and control research, Gréhaigne & Godbout (1995) proposed that games involve teams operating as competency networks engaged in high strategy sports (e.g., invasion or net/wall games) against opponents in a contest and that learning occurs for both individuals and teams.

Four components of games (cooperation with teammates, opposition to opponents, attacking opponents' space, and defending a team's own space) can be taken as highly sophisticated goal structures using forms of declarative and procedural knowledge (Gréhaigne, Godbout, & Bouthier, 1999). Gréhaigne et al. reiterate the importance of strategic and tactical knowledge as key components of expert game play. They assert that these can be taught by carefully structuring learning environments to facilitate use of players' knowledge structures when representing and solving problems related to game play, thus expanding their knowledge structures. They also explored more specifically the role of decision-making during game play (Gréhaigne, Godbout, & Bouthier, 2001), concluding that decisions are grounded in dynamic, fluid configurations of game play related to player positions and the location of the ball. These concepts are amenable to an information-processing interpretation in that players use appropriate cues from the environment (e.g., game play) to activate portions of their knowledge structure so that appropriate responses are selected and executed.

Motor learning researchers have used the information-processing perspective to study expert–novice sport performance. The following is a summary of their research findings.

- Expert performers plan, while novice performers "wait and see."
- Expert performers continuously monitor relevant current and past responses and build and modify their game status. Novice performers react to game events rather than plan for response selection (McPherson, 1999a; McPherson, 1999b).
- Expert performers use a specific approach to problem solving that is highly contextual while novice performers use a global approach to problem solving (McPherson & Thomas, 1989).
- Expert performers process information at a deeper, more tactical level, while novice performers process events in the environment or surface features of a game situation (McPherson & Thomas, 1989).
- Expert performers make faster and more accurate decisions, while novice performers have slower access to the information needed to make accurate decisions.
- Expert performers have specialized search and retrieval abilities (if-then-do statements) from game situations and long-term memories, while novice performers do not have these abilities or the game experiences to draw from in their long-term memories (Rink, French, & Tjeerdsma, 1996; McPherson & Thomas, 1989).
- Expert performers will (a) have high success at performing skills correctly during games, (b) perform effortlessly and more automatically (i.e., make it look easy), (c) show greater consistency and adaptability in performing movement patterns, and (d) be better at monitoring their own performance as well as detecting and correcting errors (Rink et al., 1996).
- In early work Thomas, French, and McPherson suggested that knowledge and decision-making processes may develop faster than motor skills (French & Thomas, 1987; McPherson & French, 1991; McPherson & Thomas, 1989). They believe now that this assertion is wrong in that knowledge and the decision-making develop much more slowly (French & McPherson, in press).
- Different instructional approaches produce different knowledge representations that influence the performers' views and interpretations of game events (French & Thomas, 1987; French, Spurgeon, & Nevett, 1995; Werner; Rink et al., 1996; French, Werner, Taylor, Hussey, Jones, 1996; McPherson & French, 1991; McPherson, 1994).

We believe that the understanding and development of learners' domain-specific knowledge provides us, as teachers and researchers, with an additional means to facilitate learning and to find out what children know about physical education at the outset of instruction and as instruction unfolds over time (Griffin & Placek, 2001). This strategy acknowledges that learners are active participants in the teaching-learning process (Weinstein & Mayer, 1986) and come to every new learning experience with some knowledge about the topic already established. In a physical education context, players' knowledge is important in building overall game skills, knowing what to do and under which conditions to do it, knowing how to perform particular motor skill components of the game, and knowing how to apply these skills tactically and strategically during game play.

Viewing the learning process with information-processing theory and research demonstrates just how complex the instructional environment is and the difficulty teachers are faced with to facilitate learning (Dodds et al., 2001). Thus, researchers need to continue to explore the various kinds of knowledge that learners hold and the interactions and relationships among those kinds of knowledge as they study various pedagogical approaches.

SITUATED LEARNING THEORY

Situated learning has also emerged as a framework to theorize and analyze pedagogical practices in physical education (Kirk & Macdonald, 1998; Kirk & MacPhail, 2002). Individuals are considered part of a holistic learning enterprise, not as acting or participating in isolation. The assumptions and organizing structures of the TDLM allows for participation to occur in a student-centered "learning curriculum" as opposed to a teacher-centered "teaching curriculum" (Lave & Wenger, 1991, p. 97). This view of a learning-centered curriculum moves the teacher off center stage and provides an opportunity for the student (i.e., learner) to help other students learn. Situated learning theory can be used to explore the potential of the TDLM as a valuable system for invasion games learning. As set forth by Kirk and Macdonald (1998), situated learning theory is conceptualized as one component of a broader constructivist theory of learning in physical education. Lave and Wenger (1991) posit that in this mode of learning, the mastering of knowledge and skills requires that novices move toward more advanced participation (full participation) in the sociocultural practices of the community.

Perkins (1999) emphasized three tenets of constructivism: the active learner, the social learner, and the creative learner. As active learners, students are not passive recipients of knowledge but are involved in tasks that stimulate decision-making, critical thinking, and problem solving. As social learners, students construct knowledge through social interaction with their peers, facilitated by their teachers. As creative learners, students are guided to discover knowledge themselves and to create their own understanding of the subject matter. Individuals draw on prior knowledge and experiences to construct knowledge.

Situated learning provides an authentic framework in which to position teaching and learning in physical education. Situated learning theory investigates the relationships among the various physical, social, and cultural dimensions of the context of learning (Lave & Wenger, 1991). Social and cultural contexts contribute to and influence what is learned and how learning takes place. Lave and Wenger (1991) discuss "legitimate peripheral participation within a community of practice" as a key concept for situated learning theory. They refer to legitimate peripheral participation as participation that occurs within sets of relationships in which "newcomers" can move toward "full participation" by being involved in particular experiences or practices, and this develops new sets of relationships. Learning is not the reception of factual knowledge or information, but rather the legitimate (genuine) peripheral (complex interplay of persons, activity, knowledge, and the social world) participation (activity toward a specific task/goal). Lave and Wenger (1991) state that legitimate peripheral participation "obtains its meaning, not in a concise definition of its boundaries, but in its multiple, theoretically generative interconnections with persons, activities, knowing, and world" (p. 121).

Kirk & Macdonald (1998) provide a useful explanation of community of practice. "We understand the notion of community of practice to refer to any collectivity or group who together contribute to shared or public practices in a particular sphere of life" (p. 380). The social and cultural situation of the teaching environment contributes significantly to what is learned and how learning takes place (Kirk & Macdonald 1998). We argue that TDLM can provide structures for situated learning to occur within a community of practice based on the meaningful, purposeful, and authentic tasks presented and practiced by students. Legitimate peripheral participation is intended to convey the sense of authentic, meaningful, and purposeful participation by students in an activity. Learning takes place in the interactive social world within social practices or interpersonal relationships that are in the process of production, reproduction, transformation, and change (Lave & Wenger, 1991). Kirk and Macdonald (1998) have argued that "school physical education may regularly and consistently *fail* to provide young people with the opportunity for legitimate peripheral participation in a community of practice of exercise, and physical recreation" (p. 382).

Constructivist and situated learning perspectives have been endorsed as providing a potentially useful reconceptualization of existing approaches to teaching and learning in physical education (Chen & Rovegno, 2000; Dodds, Griffin, & Placek, 2001; Ennis, 2000; Rovegno & Bandhauer, 1997; Kirk & Macdonald, 1998; Rovegno & Kirk, 1995). TDLM has the potential to represent situated learning within a social constructivist theoretical framework.

Guiding Pedagogical Principles

Practitioners need to take into account several pedagogical considerations when implementing the TDLM: (a) The teacher/coach is a facilitator, (b) students are active learners, (c) students work in small groups and with modified games, (d) learning activities are authentic and developmentally appropriate, (e) learning activities are interesting and challenging, and (f) students are held accountable (Dyson, Griffin, & Hastie, 2004).

- **The teacher or coach as a facilitator.** As the facilitator, the teacher sets problems or goals, and students are given an opportunity to seek solutions to these problems. Solutions to the problem are identified through a questioning process, and these solutions then become the focus of a situated practice. The teacher also facilitates the practice by either simplifying or challenging students based on their abilities. In this way the teacher is working with the students' prior knowledge to develop new knowledge. The teacher guides the instruction and curriculum as a facilitator of learning.
- **Students are active learners.** In TDLM students have a high rate of engagement. Students take responsibility for organization and management and take on leadership roles. Teachers delegate responsibility so that more students can talk and work together on multiple learning tasks. Therefore students have positions of responsibility. The teacher is not at the center of instruction and students are active learners, creative learners, and social learners (Perkins, 1999).

- **Students work in groups or modified games**. Grouping is usually heterogeneous in small groups or teams. The behaviors required in cooperative small groups are radically different from those required in traditional classroom settings (Cohen, 1994). Modifying the games allows students to practice their skills and decision-making in "real," game-like situations. Having the teacher emphasize authentic performance puts students in an active learning situation (Darling-Hammond, 1997). For an activity to be considered authentic in physical education, it must involve some form of observable performance (Wiggins, 1993).
- **Learning activities are interesting and challenging**. When learning activities are either interesting or challenging to students, they are more likely to be satisfying or even enjoyable. The discovery of solutions to various learning activities requires that students contribute to the group or team task.
- **Students are held accountable**. Assessment is an ongoing part of instruction, and students are provided with continuous feedback for reflecting on and problem solving about games or physical activity experiences. Assessment should be authentic and aligned with specific tactical problems to be solved.

IMPLICATIONS FOR LEARNING AND INSTRUCTION

From the research base using the information-processing perspective, French and McPherson (2004) provide what they refer to as "best guess approaches" to sport-related games learning. First, teachers and coaches should design game play situations so that students must make decisions that should be repeated many times. Second, teachers and coaches should use questions to gain insight and information from students about what they are processing or not processing. Finally, we have argued that situated learning, a community of practice based on the meaningful, purposeful, and authentic learning activities presented and practiced by students, also provides a strong theory from which to explore a games learning teaching system (Kirk & Macdonald, 1998; Kirk & MacPhail, 2002; Lave & Wenger, 1991).

Much more research and development work is needed to understand how to facilitate the development of game knowledge. A challenging but important question is to explore what types of learning situations (i.e., games or practice) elicit what types of improvement in game performance (i.e., decision-making and execution) (French & McPherson, 2004).

Application of a better theory for games learning has implications for sport pedagogy researchers, teachers, and coaches and for the students. First, application of theory may add to the limited knowledge of how teachers, coaches, and students learn games and will aid in curriculum development and better ways of teaching games.

Teachers and coaches who know more about the prior knowledge their students or players bring to class have better opportunities to provide a quality learning environment that extends and deepens that knowledge during instruction. When teachers and coaches understand students' knowledge structures, which include nodes and relationships among them, they can build on what students already know, making bridges to new learning. Physical educators and coaches, whose curricula largely rely on games in various forms (Rovegno, Nevett, & Barbiarz, 2001), could thus design learning tasks that challenge students to increase and better connect their knowledge of rules, strategies and tactics, motor skill selection and execution, and decision-making in games contexts.

Physical education teachers and coaches can consider students' prior knowledge to identify gaps in students' knowledge structures so that instruction and practice opportunities can be tailored to address these. For example, teachers who know students lack a particular aspect of tactical knowledge might design and cater instruction to fill this knowledge void.

Finally, a better theory for games learning has implications for students and players. As physical education teachers and coaches learn how to access students' prior knowledge structures, they will have a more complete picture of where gaps exist within groups of students' knowledge, and they may become more adept at providing challenging learning environments that will facilitate students' learning and skillfulness. As students gain expertise in games, they are more likely to enjoy the activity and to include participation outside school contexts in their daily lives, thus strengthening the possibility of lifelong participation in games and other physical activities.

Bibliography

AEEPS (1977). Sports co n° 3. Paris : Amicale ENSEPS.

Alexander, P., & Judy, J. (1988). The interaction of domain-specific and strategic knowledge in academic performance. *Review of Educational Research, 58,* 375–404.

Ali, A. H. (1988). Statistical analysis of tactical movement patterns in association football. In T. Reilly, A. Lees, K. Davids, & W. J. Murphy (Eds.) *Science and football* (pp. 302–308). London : E. & F.N. SPON.

Ali, A.H., & Farraly, M. (1990). An analysis of patterns of play in soccer. *Science and football, 3,* 37–44.

Allal, L., Cardinet, J., & Perrenoud, P. (1979). *L'évaluation formative dans un enseignement différencié* [Formative assessment in a differentiated teaching]. Berne: Peter Lang.

Allison, S., & Thorpe, R. (1997). A comparison of the effectiveness of two approaches to teaching games within physical education. A skill approach versus a game for understanding approach. *British Journal of Physical Education,* Autumn 1997.

Almond, L. (1986a) Primary and secondary rules in games. In R. Thorpe, D. Bunker, & L. Almond (Eds.), *Rethinking games teaching* (pp. 73–74). Loughborough, England: Loughborough University of Technology.

Almond, L. (1986b) Reflecting on themes: A games classification. In R. Thorpe, D. Bunker, & L. Almond (Eds.), *Rethinking games teaching* (pp. 71–72). Loughborough, England: Loughborough University of Technology.

Amicale des Anciens Élèves de l'ENSEPS. (1966). Des colloques de Vichy 1964–1965. *Éducation Physique et Sport, 78,* 19–73.

Anderson, J. R. (1976). *Language, memory, and thought.* Hillsdale, NJ: Erlbaum.

Andreewsky, E. (1991). *Systémique & cognition* [Systemics & cognition]. Paris: Dunod.

Anzieu, D., Martin, J. Y. (1968). *La dynamique des groupes restreints.* Paris: PUF.

Atlan, H. (1979). *Entre le cristal et la fumée.* Paris: Seuil.

Bailey, L., & Almond, L. (1983). Creating change: By creating games? In L. Spackman (Ed.), *Teaching games for understanding* (pp. 56–59). Cheltenham, England: The College of St. Paul and St. Mary.

Barbier, J. M. (1996). *Savoirs théoriques et savoirs d'action.* Paris: PUF.

Barrow, H. M., McGee, R., & Tritschler, K. A. (1989). *Practical measurement in physical education and sport* (4th ed.). Philadelphia: Lea & Febiger.

Barth, B. (1994). Strategie und Taktik im Wettkampfsport. *Leistungssport, 3,* 4–14.

Baumgartner, T. A., & Jackson, A. S. (1991). *Measurement and evaluation in physical education and exercise science* (4th ed.). Dubuque, IA: Wm. C. Brown.

165

Bayer, C. (1979). *L'enseignement des jeux sportifs collectifs* [The teaching of team sport games]. Paris: Vigot.

Bernard, M. (1963). Une interprétation dialectique de la dynamique de l'équipe. *Éducation Physique et Sport, 62-63*, 7–11.

Bertalanffy, L. V. (1972). *Théorie générale des systèmes*. Paris: Dunod.

Blomquist, M.T., Luhtanen, P., Laakso, L., & Keskinen, E. (2000). Validation of a video-based game–understanding test procedure in badmitton. *Journal of Teaching in Physical Education, 19*, 325–337.

Boudreau, P. (1987). *L'évaluation par les pairs. Une étude de sa justesse et de son influence sur l'apprentissage d'une activité physique (hockey)* [Peer assessment. A study on its reliability and its impact on the learning of a physical activity (hockey)]. Unpublished master's thesis, Université Laval, Québec, Canada.

Bourdieu, P. (1972). *Esquisse d'une théorie de la pratique*. Genèva, Switzerland: Droz.

Bourdieu, P. (1980). *Le sens pratique*. Paris: Minuit.

Bouthier, D. (1984). *Sports collectifs: Contribution à l'analyse de l'activité et éléments pour une formation tactique essentielle. L'exemple du rugby* [Team sports: Contribution to the analysis of the activity and elements of essential tactical learning]. Paris: INSEP.

Bouthier, D. (1986). Comparaison expérimentale des effets de différents modèles didactiques des sports collectifs [Experimental comparison of the effects of different didactic models in team sports]. In *E.P.S.-Contenus et didactique* (pp. 85–89). Paris: SNEP.

Bouthier, D. (1988). *Les conditions cognitives de la formation d'actions sportives collectives.* [Cognitive conditions for learning in team sports]. Unpublished doctoral dissertation, Université Paris V, Paris, France.

Bouthier, D. (1989). Les conditions cognitives de la formation d'actions sportives collectives. [Cognitive conditions for learning in team sports]. *Le Travail Humain, 52*(2), 175–182.

Bouthier, D. (1993). *L'approche technologique en STAPS; représentations et actions en didactique des APS.* [Technological approach in STAPS; Representation and actions in sport and physical activities]. Habilitation à diriger les recherches, Université de Paris 11, Orsay, France.

Bouthier, D., & Durey, A. (1994). Technologie des APS. *Impulsion, 1*, 95–120.

Bouthier, D., & Reitchess, S. (1984). *Contenus et évaluation en sports collectifs*. Paris: C.R.D.P.

Bouthier, D., & Savoyant, A. (1984). A contribution to the learning of a collective action; The counter attack in rugby. *Journal of Sport Psychology, 15*(1), 25–34.

Bouthier, D., David, B., & Eloi, S. (1994). Analysis of representations and patterns of tactical decisions in team games: A methodological approach. In J. Nistch & R. Seiler (Eds.), *Motor control and motor learning* (pp. 126–134). Sankt Augustin: Academic Verlag.

Bouthier, D., Pastré, P., & Samurçay, A. (1995). Le développement des compétences. Analyse du travail et didactique professionnelle. [The development of competencies. Analysis of work and professional didactics]. *Éducation Permanente, 123*.

Brackenridge, C. (1979). *Games: Classification and analysis*. Conference presented to the Kirkless Teachers.

Bransford, J. D., Brown, A. L., & Cocking, R. R. (Eds.). (2000). *How people learn—Brain, mind, experience and school*. Washington, D. C.: National Academy Press.

Brechbuhl, J., Bronckart, J. P., & Joannisse, R. (1988). Contribution à une didactique du sport [Contribution to sport didactics]. *Université de Genève. Cahier de la section des sciences de l'éducation-Pratiques et théorie, 49*, 1–145.

Brousseau, G. (1986). *Fondements et méthodes en didactique des mathématiques*. Grenoble, France: La Pensée Sauvage.

Brown, E. W. (1982). Visual evaluation techniques for skill analysis. *Journal of Physical Education and Recreation, 53*(1), 21–26, 29.

Bunker, D. & Thorpe, R (1982). A model for teaching of games in the secondary schools. *Bulletin of Physical Education, 10*, 9–16.

Bunker, D., & Thorpe, R. (1983). A model for the teaching of games in secondary schools. *Bulletin of Physical Education, 18*(1), 5–8.

Bunker, D., & Thorpe, R. (1986). Is there a need to reflect on our games teaching? In R. Thorpe, D. Bunker, & L. Almond (Eds.), *Rethinking games teaching* (pp. 25–33). Loughborough, England: Loughborough University of Technology.

Bunker, D., & Thorpe, R. (1986a). The curriculum model. In R. Thorpe, D. Bunker, & L. Almond (Eds.), *Rethinking games teaching* (pp. 7–10). Loughborough, England: Loughborough University of Technology.

Butler, J., Griffin, L., Lombardo, B., & Nastasi, R. (2003). *Teaching for understanding in physical education and sport.* Oxon Hill: AAPHERD Publications.

Caillois, R. (1961). Man, play and games. New York: Free Press of Glencoe.

Cam, Y., Crunelle, J., Giana, E., Grosgeorge, B., & Labiche, J. (1979). *Basket-ball. Mémento du CPS FSGT.* Paris: Sport et Plein Air.

Cardinet, J. (1986). *Évaluation scolaire et mesure.* Brussels: De Boeck.

Caron, J., & Pelchat, C. (1975). Apprentissage des sports collectifs, hockey et basket [Learning of team sports, hockey and basketball].Québec : PUQ.

Carron, A. V. (1988). *Group in sport: Theoretical and practical issues.* London, Ontario: Spodym.

Caverni, J. P. (1988). La verbalisation comme source d'observables pour l'étude du fonctionnement cognitif [Verbalization as an observationable source of information about cognitive process]. In J.P. Caverni, C. Bastien, P. Mendelsohn, & G. Tiberghien (Eds.), *Psychologie cognitive: Modèles et méthodes* [Cognitive psychology: Models and methods] (pp. 253–273). Grenoble, France: Presses Universitaires.

Caverni, J. P., Bastien, C., Mendelsohn, P., & Tiberghien, G. (1988). *Psychologie cognitive: Modèles et méthodes.* Grenoble, France: Presses Universitaires.

Chamberlain, C. J., & Coelho, A. J. (1993). The perceptual side of actions: Decision making in sport. In J. J. Starkes and F. Allard (Eds.), *Cognitive issues in motor expertise* (pp. 135–157). Elsevier Science Publishers B.V.

Chen, W., & Rovegno, I. (2000). Examination of expert teachers' constructivist-orientated teaching practices using a movement approach to physical education. *Research Quarterly for Exercise and Sport, 71,* 357–372.

Cobb, P. (1986). Making mathematics: Children's learning and the constructivist tradition. *Harvard Educational Review, 56,* 301–306.

Cohen, E. G. (1994). Restructuring in the classroom: Conditions for productive small groups. *Review of Educational Research, 64,* 1–35.

Cohen, E. G., & Lotan, R. A. (1997). *Working for equity in heterogeneous classrooms: Sociological theory in practice.* New York: Teachers College Press.

Corbin, C.B. (2000). Physical activity for everyone: What every physical educator should know about promoting lifelong physical activity. *Journal of Teaching in Physical Education, 21,* 128–144.

Darling-Hammond, L. (1997). *The right to learn.* San Francisco, Jossey-Bass.

Dassé, B. (1986). *Étude sur la capacité d'élèves à mesurer des habiletés motrices de leurs pairs et influence sur l'apprentissage.* [A study of students' capacity of assessing their peers' motor skills and impact on learning]. Unpublished master's thesis, Université Laval, Québec, Canada.

David, B. (1993). *Place et rôle des représentations dans la mise en oeuvre didactique d'une activité physique et sportive: L'exemple du rugby.* Thèse (nouveau régime). Université Paris-Sud, Paris, France.

Davids, K., Handford, C., and Williams, M. (1994). The natural alternative to cognitive theories of motor behaviour: An invitation for interdisciplinary research in sport science? *Journal of Sports Sciences, 12,* 495–528.

Davisse, A., & Louveau, C. (1991). *Sports, école, société: La part des femmes.* Paris: Actio.

De Montmollin, M. (1986). *L'intelligence de la tâche: éléments d'ergonomie cognitive.* Bern, Switzerland: Peter Lang.

Deleplace, R. (1966). *Le rugby* [Rugby Union]. Paris: Armand Colin Bourrelier.

Deleplace, R. (1979). *Rugby de mouvement—Rugby total* [Rugby in movement—Total rugby]. Paris: Éducation Physique et Sport.

Deleplace, R. (1992). Phases statiques: Lancement du jeu par les lignes arrières. In AEEPS, Marciac 91 (Ed.), *Les forums du rugby* (pp. 11–27). Paris: AEEPS.

Deleplace, R. (1995). *Logique du jeu et conséquences sur l'entraînement à la tactique.* Communication orale "Colloque sport collectif," Paris: INSEP.

Deriaz, D. & Poussin, B. (2001). Plan d'Études: Éducation physique. Genève: cycle d'orientation de l'enseignement secondaire, département de l'Instruction Publique.

Deriaz, D., Poussin, B., & Gréhaigne, J. F. (1998). Le débat d'idées. *Éducation physique et sport, 273,* 80–82.

Desrosiers, P., Genet-Volet, Y., & Godbout, P. (1997). Teachers' assessment practices viewed through the instruments used in physical education classes. *Journal of Teaching in Physical Education, 16,* 211–228.

Diaz, J. C. (1983). *Problèmes posés par l'apprentissage du rugby chez de jeunes enfants, l'exemple d'une situation de un contre un.* Mémoire de Maîtrise en STAPS. Université Paris V, Paris, France.

Dodds, P., Griffin, L. L., & Placek, J. H. (2001). A selected review of the literature on the development of learners' domain-specific knowledge. *Journal of Teaching in Physical Education [Monograph], 20,* 301–313.

Dugrand, M. (1985). Approches théorique, expérimentale et clinique de l'enseignement du football. L'exemple au Sénégal. Thèse de troisième cycle, Université de Caen, Caen, France.

Dugrand, M. (1989). *Le football: De la transparence à la complexité* [Soccer: From transparency to complexity]. Paris: PUF.

Durand, M. (1989). Transversalité et progressivité des apprentissages en Éducation Physique et Sportive. *Actes de l'Université d'Été de Dijon,* September 1989.

Dyson, B., Griffin, L. L., & Hastie, P. (in press). Theoretical and pedagogical considerations for implementing sport education, tactical games, and cooperative learning instructional models. *Quest.*

Ennis, C.D. (2000). Canaries in the coal mine: Responding to disengaged students using theme-based curricula. *Quest, 52,* 119–130.

Ericsson, K. A. (1996). *The road to excellence: The acquisition of expert performance in the arts and science, sports, and games.* Mahwah, NJ: Lawrence Elbaum.

Ericsson, K. A., & Charness, N. (1994). Expert Performance. Its structure and acquisition. *American Psychology, 49,* 725–747.

Ericsson, K. A., & Simon, H. A. (1993). *Protocol analysis: Verbal reports as data* (rev. ed.). Cambridge, MA: MIT Press.

Ericsson, K. A., Krampe, R. T. & Tesch-Römer, C. (1993). The role of deliberate practice in the acquisition of expert performance. *Psychological Review, 100,* 3, 363–406.

Famose, J. P. (1996). Les recherches actuelles sur l'apprentissage moteur [Present research on motor learning]. *Dossier EPS, 28.*

French K. E., & McPherson, S. L. (1999). Adaptations in response selection processes used during sport competition with increasing age and expertise. *International Journal of Sport Psychology, 30,* 173–193.

French, K. E., & McPherson, S. L. (2004). The development of expertise. In M. R. Weiss (Ed.), *Developmental Sport and Exercise Psychology: A Lifespan Perspective.* Morgantown, WV: Fitness Information Technology.

French, K., & Thomas, J. (1987). The relation of knowledge development to children's basketball performance. *Journal of Sport Psychology, 9,* 15–32.

French, K., Spurgeon, J., & Nevett, M. (1995). Expert-novice differences in cognitive and skill execution components of youth baseball performance. *Research Quarterly for Exercise and Sport, 66,* 194–201.

French, K. E., Werner, P. H., Taylor, K., Hussey, K.,& Jones, J. (1996). The effects of a 6-week unit of tactical, skill, or combined tactical and skill instruction on badminton performance of ninth-grade students. *Journal of Teaching in Physical Education, 15,* 439–463.

French, K., Nevett, M., Spurgeon, J., Graham, K., Rink, J., & McPherson, S. (1996). Knowledge and problem solution in youth baseball. *Research Quarterly for Exercise and Sport, 67,* 386–395.

Gardner, H. (1992). Assessment in context: The alternative to standardized testing. In B.R. Gifford, & M.C. O'Connor (Eds.), *Changing assessments-Alternative view of aptitude, achievement and instruction* (pp. 77–119). Boston: Kluwer Academic Publishers.

Giordan, A., & De Vecchi, G. (1987). Les origines du savoir. Neuchâtel: Delachaux & Niestlé.

Godbout, P. (1990). Observational strategies for the rating of motor skills: Theoretical and practical implications. In M. Lirette, C. Paré, J. Dessureault, & M. Piéron (Eds.), *Physical education and coaching—Present state and outlook for the future* (pp. 209– 221).

Goirand, P. (1993). Règles ou principes d'action en EPS [Rules or principles of action in physical education]? Lyon, France: *Spirales 6,* 143–159.

Good, T. (1996). Teaching effects and teacher evaluation. In J. Sikula, T.J. Buttery, & E. Guyton (Eds.), *Handbook of research on teacher education* (2nd edition, pp. 617–665). New York: Simon & Schuster.

Good, T., & Brophy, J. (1994). *Looking in classroom* (6th ed.). New York: Harper Collins.

Gréhaigne, J. F. (1988). Game systems in soccer. In T. Reilly, A. Lees, K. Davids, & W. J. Murphy (Eds.), *Science and Football* (pp. 316–321). London: E. & F.N. SPON.

Gréhaigne, J. F. (1989). *Football de mouvement. Vers une approche systémique du jeu* [Soccer in movement. Towards a systemic approach of the game]. Unpublished doctoral dissertation. Université de Bourgogne, Dijon, France.

Gréhaigne, J. F. (1992). *L'organisation du jeu en football* [The organisation of play in soccer]. Paris: ACTIO.

Gréhaigne, J. F. (1992a). Modélisation pondérée de l'attaque du but en football. In M. Laurent J.F. Marini, R. Pfister, & P. Therme (Eds.), *Les performances motrices: Approche multidisciplinaire.* (pp. 521–529). Paris: Actio/Université d'Aix—Marseille II.

Gréhaigne, J. F. (1992b). Les représentations du jeu en sport collectif et leurs conséquences sur l'apprentissage [Representations of play in team sports and their consequences for learning]. In J. Colomb (Ed.), *Recherche en didactique: Contribution à la formation des maîtres* (pp. 148–158). Paris: INRP.

Gréhaigne, J. F. (1994). Analyse comparative de deux types d'enseignement des sports collectifs : approche centrée sur la technique et approche centrée sur le jeu. *Rapport de Recherche.* IUFM de Franche-Comté.

Gréhaigne, J. F. (1994a). Quelques aspects bibliographiques concernant l'enseignement des sports collecifs à l'école. *E.P.S., Dossier 17,* 12–15.

Gréhaigne, J. F. (1995). Des exemples de pratiques d'évaluation pour les jeux sportifs collectifs [Examples of assessment practices in team sports]. *Revue de l'Éducation Physique, 35,* 125–134.

Gréhaigne, J. F. (1996). Les règles d'actions: Un support pour les apprentissages [Action rules: A support for learning]. *Éducation Physique et Sport, 265,* 71–73.

Gréhaigne, J. F. (1997). *Modélisation du jeu de football et traitement didactique des jeux sportifs collectifs* [Modeling of play in soccer and didactic treatment of team sports]. Habilitation à diriger les recherches, Université de Paris 11, Orsay, France.

Gréhaigne, J. F., & Bouthier, D. (1994). Analyse des évolutions entre deux configurations du jeu en football. *Science et Motricité, 24,* 44–52.

Gréhaigne, J. F., & Cadopi, M. (1990). Apprendre en éducation physique. In AEEPS (Ed.), *Éducation physique et didactique des APS* (pp. 17–24). Paris: AEEPS.

Gréhaigne, J. F., & Godbout P. (1995). Tactical knowledge in team sports from a constructivist and cognitivist perspective. *Quest, 47*, 490–505.

Gréhaigne, J. F., & Godbout, P. (1997). The teaching of tactical knowledge in team sports. *Journal of Canadian Association for Physical Education, Recreation and Dance, 63*(4), 10–15.

Gréhaigne, J. F., & Godbout, P. (1998). Formative assessment in team sports with a tactical approach. *Journal of Physical Education, Recreation and Dance, 69*(1), 46–51.

Gréhaigne, J. F., & Godbout, P. (1999). Observation, critical thinking and transformation: Three key elements for a constructivist perspective of the learning process in team sports. In R.S. Feingold, C.R. Rees, G.T. Barrette, L. Fiorentino, S. Virgilio, & E. Kowalski (Eds.), *Education for life* (pp. 109–118). Garden City, NY: Adelphi University.

Gréhaigne, J. F., & Godbout, P. (1999a). La prise de décision de l'élève en sport collectif. In J.F. Gréhaigne, N. Mahut, & D. Marchal (Eds.), *Qu'apprennent les élèves en faisant des activités physiques et sportives ?* [CD-ROM]. (Dossier Symposia, 2). Besançon: IUFM, Université de Franche-Comté.

Gréhaigne, J. F., & Guillon, R. (1991). Du bon usage des règles d'action [Making good use of action rules]. *Echanges et controverses, 4*, 43–66.

Gréhaigne, J. F., & Laroche, J. Y. (1994). Quelques fondements et présupposés théoriques d'une démarche [Some theoretical bases and assumptions of an approach]. *E.P.S., Dossier 17*, 12–15.

Gréhaigne, J. F., & Roche, J. (1990). Quelques questions à propos du football [A few questions concerning soccer].In AEEPS (Ed.), *Education physique et didactique des APS* (pp. 63–72). Paris: AEEPS.

Gréhaigne, J. F., & Roche, J. (1993). Les sports collectifs au bac [Team sports in "baccalauréat"]. *Education Physique et Sport, 240*, 80–83.

Gréhaigne, J. F., Billard, M., & Laroche, J. Y. (1999). *L'enseignement des jeux sportifs collectifs à l'école. Conception, construction, évaluation.* Brussels: De Boeck.

Gréhaigne, J. F., Bouthier, D., & David, B. (1997). Dynamic-system analysis of opponent relationships in collective actions in soccer. *Journal of Sports Sciences, 15*, 137–149.

Gréhaigne, J. F., Godbout, P., & Bouthier, D. (1997). Performance assessment in team sports. *Journal of Teaching in Physical Education, 16*, 500–516.

Gréhaigne, J. F., Godbout, P., & Bouthier, D. (1999). The foundations of tactics and strategy in team sports. *Journal of Teaching in Physical Education, 18*, 159–174.

Gréhaigne, J. F., Godbout, P., & Bouthier, D. (2001). The teaching and learning of decision making in team sports. *Quest, 53*, 59–76.

Gréhaigne, J. F., Billard, M., Guillon, R., & Roche, J. (1988). Vers une autre conception de l'enseignement des sports collectifs [Towards an other view of the teaching of team sports]. In G. Bui-Xuan (Ed.), *Méthodologie et didactique de l'éducation physique et sportive* (pp. 155–172). Clermont-Ferrand, France: AFRAPS.

Gréhaigne, J. F., Richard, J. F., Mahut, N., & Griffin, L. (2002). Reflections on player competencies in team sport. *Journal of Sport Pedagogy, 8* (2), 22–37.

Griffin, L., & Placek, J. (2001). The understanding and development of learners domain-specific knowledge: Introduction. *Journal of Teaching in Physical Education, 20*(4), 299–300.

Griffin, L., Mitchell, S., & Oslin, J. (1997). *Teaching sport concepts and skills: A tactical games approach.* Champaign, IL: Human Kinetics.

Hanson, P. G., & Lubin, B. (1988). Team building as group development. In W.B. Reddy, & K. Jamison (Eds.), *Team building: Blueprints for productivity and satisfaction* (pp. 76–78). Alexandria, VA: National Institute for Applied Behavioral Science.

Harrison, J. M., Preece, L. A., Blakemore, C. L., Richards, R. P., Wilkinson C., & Felligham, G. W. (1999). Effects of two instructional models—skill teaching and mastery learning—on skill developpement, knowledge, self-effcacity, and game play in volleyball. *Journal of Teaching in Physical Education, 19,* 157–171.

Helsen, W., Starkes, J., & Hodges, N. (1998). Team sports and the theory of deliberate practice. *Journal of Sport and Exercise Psychology, 20,* 12–34.

Hoc, J. M., & Leplat, J. (1983). Evaluation of different modalities of verbalization in a sorting task. *Journal of Verbal Learning and Verbal Behavior, 3,* 187–198.

Holt, N. L., Strean, W. B., & Bengoechea, E. G. (2002). Expanding the teaching games for understanding model: New avenues for future research and practice. *Journal of Teaching in Physical Education, 21,* 162–176.

Houdé, O. (1992). *Catégorisation et développement cognitif.* Paris: PUF.

Hughes, C. (1980). *The football association coaching book of soccer tactics and skills.* London: Queen Anne Press.

Huizinga, J. (1951). Homo ludens, essai sur la fonction social du jeu. Paris: Gallimard.

Janis, I.L., & Feshbach, S. (1953). Effect of fear-arousing communication. *Journal of Abnormal and Social Psychology,* 48.

Kirk, D. (1983). Theoretical guidelines for "teaching for understanding." In L. Spackman (Ed.), *Teaching games for understanding* (pp. 80–83). Cheltenham, England: The College of St. Paul and St. Mary.

Kirk, D., & Macdonald, D. (1998). Situated learning in physical education. *Jounal of Teaching in Physical Education, 17,* 376–378.

Kirk, D., & MacPhail, A. (2002). Teaching games for understanding and situated learning: Rethinking the Bunker-Thorpe model. *Journal of Teaching in Physical Education, 21,* 177–192.

Lambert, N. M., & McCombs, B. L. (Eds.) (1998). *How students learn—Reforming schools through learner-centered education.* Washington, D.C.: American Psychological Association.

Laroche, J. Y., & Gréhaigne, J. F. (1995, October/November). *Utiliser un nomogramme avec des groupes mixtes. Quelle validité pour une évaluation en volley-ball.* Communication affichée: Journées d'automne de l'ACAPS, Guadeloupe.

Lave, & Wenger. (1991). *Situated learning: Legitimate peripheral participation.* New York: Cambridge University Press.

Leontiev, A. (1976). Le développement du psychisme: Problèmes [The development of psyche]. Paris: Éditions sociales.

Leplat, J. (1995). A propos des compétences incorporées. *Education Permanente, 123,* 101–123.

Mahlo, F. (1974). *Acte tactique en jeu* [Tactical action in play]. Paris: Vigot. (Originally published in German in 1969.)

Mahut, N., Nachon, M., Mahut, B., & Gréhaigne, J. F. (2000, October). *Illettrisme et apprentissage en E.P.S. L'acte moteur en débat.* Symposium conducted at the Colloque sur l'illettrisme, Reims, France.

Malglaive, G. (1990). *Enseigner à des adultes* [Teaching to adults]. Paris: PUF.

Marin, J. C. (1993). Règles d'action, histoire d'une notion [Action rules, the story of a notion]. Lyon, France: *Spirales 6,* 103–109.

McBride, R. E. (1991). Critical thinking—An overview with implications for physical education. *Journal of Teaching in Physical Education, 11,* 112–125.

McGee, R. (1984). Evaluation of processes and products. In B.J. Logsdon, K. R. Barrett, M. Ammons, M. R. Broer, L. E. Halverson, R. McGee, & M. A. Roberton (Eds.), *Physical education for children: A focus on the teaching process* (2nd ed., pp. 356–421). Philadelphia: Lea & Febiger.

McMorris, T. (1999). Cognitive development and the acquisition of decision-making skills. *International Journal of Sport Psychology, 30,* 151–172.

McMorris, T., & Beazeley, A. (1997). Performance of experienced and inexperienced of soccer players on soccer specific tests of recall, visual search and decision-making. *Journal of Human Movement Studies, 33,* 1–13.

McMorris, T., & Graydon, J. (1997). The contribution of the research literature to the understanding of decision making in team games. *Journal of Human Movement Studies, 33,* 69–90.

McMorris, T., & MacGillivary, W. W. (1988). An investigation into the relationship between field independence and decision making in soccer. In T. Reilly, A. Lees, K. Davids, & W. J. Murphy (Eds.), *Science and Football* (pp. 552–557). London: Spon.

McPherson, S. L. (1993). Knowledge representation and decision making in sport. In J.J. Starkes and F. Allard (Eds.), *Cognitive issues in motor expertise* (pp. 159–188). Elsevier Science Publishers B.V.

McPherson, S. L. (1993a). The influence of player experience on problem solving during batting preparation in baseball. *Journal of Sport & Exercice Psychology, 15,* 304–325.

McPherson, S. L. (1994). The development of sport expertise: Mapping the tactical domain. *Quest, 46,* 223–240.

McPherson, S. L. (1999a). Expert-novice differences in performance skills and problem representations of youth and adults during tennis competition. *Research Quarterly for Exercise and Sport, 70,* 233–251.

McPherson, S. L. (1999b). Tactical differences in problem representations and solutions in collegiate varsity and beginner women tennis players. *Research Quarterly for Exercise and Sport, 70,* 369–384.

McPherson, S., & French, K. (1991). Changes in cognitive strategies and motor skills in tennis. *Journal of Sport & Exercise Psychology, 13,* 26–41.

McPherson, S., & Thomas, J. (1989). Relation of knowledge and performance in boys' tennis: Age and expertise. *Journal of Experimental Child Psychology, 48,* 190–211.

Mérand, R. (1977). *L'éducateur face à la haute performance olympique* [The educator faced with high olympic performance]. Paris: Sport et Plein Air.

Mérand, R. (1984). Contribution à l'évaluation des connaissances et des capacités d'analyse des activités pratiquées [Contribution to the assessment of knowledge and of analysis capacities of physical activities]. In *L'évaluation en E.P.S.* (pp. 206–207). Paris: SNEP.

Mitchell, S. A. (1996). Improving invasion game performance. *Journal of Physical Education, Recreation and Dance, 67*(3), 30–33.

Mitchell, S. A., Griffin, L. L., & Oslin, J. L. (1994). Tactical awareness as a developmentally appropriate focus for the teaching of games in elementary and secondary physical education. *The Physical Educator, 51*(1), 21–28.

Mitchell, S. A., Oslin, J. L., & Griffin, L. L. (1995). The effects of two instructional approaches on game performance. *Pedagogy in practice—Teaching and coaching in physical education and sports, 1,* 36–48.

Morin, E. (1986) *La connaissance de la connaissance.* Paris: Seuil.

Nevett, M. E., & French, K. E. (1997). The development of sport-specific planning, rehearsal, and updating of plans during defensive youth baseball game performance. *Research Quarterly for Exercise and Sport, 68,* 203–214.

Nougier, V., & Rossi, B. (1999). The development of expertise in the orienting of attention. *International Journal of Sport Psychology, 30,* 246–260.

Nuttin, J. (1985). *Théorie de la motivation humaine: Du besoin au projet d'action* [Human motivation theory: From need to action project]. Paris: Presses Universitaires de France.

Oslin, J. L., Mitchell, S. A., & Griffin, L. (1998). The Game Performance Assessment Instrument (GPAI): Development and preliminary validation. *Journal of Teaching in Physical Education, 17,* 231–243.

Parker, G. M. (1990). *Team players and teamwork: The new competitive business strategy.* San Francisco: Jossey-Bass.

Parlebas, P. (1976). Les universaux du jeu sportif collectif, la modélisation du jeu sportif. *Éducation Physique et Sport, 141,* 33.

Piaget, J. (1967). *Biologie et connaissances* [Biology and knowledge]. Paris: Gallimard.

Piaget, J. (1971). *Biology and knowledge: An essay on the relations between organic regulations and cognitive processes.* (B. Walsh, Trans.). Chicago: University of Chicago Press.

Piaget, J. (1974a). *Réussir et comprendre* [Succeeding and understanding]. Paris: PUF.

Piaget, J. (1974b). *La prise de conscience* [Sudden awareness]. Paris: PUF.

Pinheiro, V. (1994). Diagnosing motor skills—A practical approach. *Journal of Physical Education, Recreation, and Dance, 65*(2), 49–54.

Perkins, D. (1999). The many faces of constructivism. *Educational Researcher, 57,* 6–11.

Plummer, O. K., & Rougeau, D. (1997). Team building magic for all. *Strategies, 10*(6), 22–24.

Rauschenbach, J. (1996). Charge! and catch coop. Two games for teaching game for play strategy. *Journal of Physical Education, Recreation and Dance, 67*(5), 49–51.

Resnick, L. B. (1987). *Education and learning to think.* Washington, D.C.: National Academy Press.

Reitchess, S. (1983). Problèmes posés par l'apprentissage d'actions collectives en rugby en utilisant une pédagogie des choix tactiques avec de jeunes enfants. Mémoire de maîtrise en STAPS. Université Paris V.

Richard, J. F. (1990). *Les activités mentales. Comprendre, raisonner, trouver des solutions* [Mental activities. Understanding, reasoning, finding solutions]. Paris: Armand Colin.

Richard, J. F. (1998). La mesure et l'évaluation de la performance en jeux et sports collectifs: La participation des élèves du primaire dans une perspective d'évaluation authentique. Unpublished doctoral dissertation. Université Laval, Québec, Canada.

Richard, J. F., Godbout, P., & Gréhaigne, J. F. (1998). The establishment of team sport performance norms for grade 5 to 8 students. *Avante, 4*(2), 1–19.

Richard, J.F., Godbout, P., & Gréhaigne, J. F. (1998a). *The precision and reliability of a performance assessment procedure in team sports.* From an unpublished doctoral dissertation. Université Laval, Québec, Canada.

Richard, J. F., Godbout, P., & Gréhaigne, J. F. (2000). Students' precision and interobserver reliability of performance assessment in team sports. *Research Quarterly for Exercise and Sport, 71*(1), 85–91.

Richard, J. F., Godbout, P., Tousignand, M., & Gréhaigne, J. F. (1999). The try-out of team-sport performance assessment procedure in elementary school and junior high school physical education classes. *Journal of Teaching in Physical Education, 18,* 336–356.

Riley, P. (1993). *The winner within: A life plan for team players.* New York: G.P. Putman's Sons.

Rink, J. E. (1996). Tactical and skill approaches to teaching sport and games [Monograph]. *Journal of Teaching in Physical Education, 15*(4).

Rink, J. E. (2001). Investigating the assumptions of pedagogy. *Journal of Teaching in Physical Education, 20,* 112–128.

Rink, J., French, K. E., & Tjeerdsma, L. (1996). Foundations for learning and instruction of sport games. *Journal of Teaching in Physical Education, 15,* 399–417.

Rioux, R., & Chapuis, G. (1967). *L'équipe dans les sports collectifs.* Paris: Vrin.

Rioux, R., & Chapuis, G. (1976). *La cohésion de l'équipe.* Paris: Vrin.

Ripoll, H. (Ed.). (1991). Information processing and decision making in sport. *International Journal of Sport Psychology, 22,* 3–4.

Ripoll, H., & Benguigui, N. (1999). Emergence of expertise in ball sports during child development. *International Journal of Sport Psychology, 30,* 235–245.

Rosnay, J. de (1975). *Le macroscope.* Paris: Seuil.

Rovegno, I. (1999, April). *What is taught and learned in physical activity programs: The role of content.* Keynote presentation at the AIESEP Conference, Besancon, France.

Rovegno, I., Nevett, M., & Babiarz, M. (2001). Learning and teaching invasion-game tactics in 4th grade: Introduction and theoretical perspective. *Journal of Teaching in Physical Education [Monograph], 20,* 341–351.

Rovegno, I., & Bandhauer, D. (1997). Norms of the school culture that facilitated teacher adoption and learning of a constructivist approach to physical education. *Journal of Teaching in Physical Education, 16,* 401–425.

Rovegno, I., & Kirk, D. (1995). Articulations and silences in social critical work on physical education: Towards a broader agenda. *Quest, 47,* 447–474.

Rumelhart, D. E., & Norman, D. A. (1978). Accretion, tuning, and restructuring: Three modes of learning. In J. W. Cotton & R. L. Klatzky (Eds.), *Semantic factors in cognition* (pp. 37–53). Hillsdale, NJ: Erlbaum.

Safrit, M. J., & Wood, T. M. (1995). *Introduction to measurement in physical education and exercise science* (3rd ed.). St. Louis, MO: Times Mirror/Mosby College Publishing.

Salmela, J. H. (1997). Détection des talents [Talent detection]. *Education Physique et Sport, 267,* 27–29.

Schmidt, R. A. (1991). *Motor learning and performance: From principles to practice.* Champaign, IL: Human Kinetics.

Schunk, D. H. (1986). Verbalization and children's self-regulated learning. *Contemporary Educational Psychology, 11,* 347–369.

Schwager, S., & Labate, C. (1993). Teaching for critical thinking in physical education. *Journal of Physical Education, Recreation and Dance, 64* (5), 24–26.

Sherif, M., & Sherif, C.W. (1979). Les relations intra et inter groupes: Une approche expéri-mentale. In W. Doise (Ed.), *Expériences entre groupes* (pp. 1–58). Paris: Mouton.

Shiffrin, R. M., & Dumais, J. T. (1981). The developmemnt of automatism. In J.R. Anderson (Ed.), *Cognitive skills and their acquisition* (pp. 111–139). Hillsdade, NJ: Lawrence Erlbaum.

Shuell, T. (1986). Cognitive conceptions of learning. *Review of Educational Research, 56,* 411–436.

Stein, J. F. (1981). *Sports d'opposition, éléments d'analyse pour une pédagogie des prises de décisions* [Opposition sports, elements of analysis for a decision making pedagogy]. Paris: INSEP.

Steinberg, G. M., Chaffin, W. M., & Singer, R. N. (1998). Mental quickness training—Drills that emphasize the development of anticipation skills in fast-paced sports. *Journal of Physical Education, Recreation and Dance, 69*(7), 37–41.

Sternberg, R. J. (1984). A theory of knowledge acquisition in the development of verbal con-cepts. *Developmental Review, 4,* 113–138.

Tennenbaum, G. (Ed.). (1999). The development of expertise in sport: nature and nurture. *International Journal of Sport Psychology, 30*(2).

Teodorescu, L. (1965). Principes pour l'étude de la tactique commune aux jeux sportifs col-lectifs [Principles for studying tactics common to team sport games]. *Revue de la S.I.E.P.E.P.S., 3,* 29–40.

Thomas, K. T., & Thomas, J. R. (1999). What squirrels in the trees predict about expert ath-letes. *International Journal of Sport Psychology, 30,* 221–234.

Thorpe, R., Bunker, D., & Almond, L. (1984). A change in focus for the teaching of game. In *Olympic Scientific Congress Proceedings, 6* (pp.163–169). Champaign, IL: Human Kinetics.

Tishman, S., & Perkins, D. (1995). Critical thinking and physical education. *Journal of Phys-ical Education, Recreation and Dance, 66*(7), 24–30.

Tsangaridou, N., & Sidentop, D. (1995). Reflective teaching: A literature review. *Quest, 47,* 212–237.

Turner, A. P., & Martinek, T. J. (1995). Teaching for understanding: A model for improving decision making during game play. *Quest, 47,* 44–63.

Van der Maren, J. M. (1999). *La recherche appliquée en pédagogie. Des modèles pour l'enseignement.* Brussels: De Boeck.

Veal, M. L. (1988). Pupil assessment perceptions and practices of secondary teachers. *Journal of Teaching in Physical Education, 7*, 327–342.

Veal, M. L. (1995). Assessment as an instructional tool. *Strategies, 8*(6), 10–15.

Vergnaud, G., Halbvacks, F., & Rouchier, A. (1978). Structure de la matière enseignée, histoire des sciences et développement conceptuel chez l'enfant [Structure of the subject matter, history of sciences and conceptual development of the child]. *Revue Française de Pédagogie, 45*, 7–18.

Villepreux, P. (1987). *Rugby de mouvement et disponibilité du joueur* [Rugby in movement and player's readiness]. Paris: Mémoire, INSEP.

Von Clausewitz, C. (1989). *De la guerre* [About war] (Rev. ed.). Paris: Lebovici.

Wade, A. (1970). *The football association guide to training and coaching*. London: EP Publishing LTD.

Walliser, B. (1977). *Systèmes et modèles. Introduction critique à l'analyse de systèmes*. Paris: Seuil.

Wallon, H. (1941). *L'évolution psychologique de l'enfant*. Paris: Armand Colin.

Weinstein, C. E., & Mayer, R. E. (1986). The teaching of learning strategies. In M. C. Wittrock (Ed.), *Handbook of research on teaching* (3rd ed., pp. 315–327). New York: Macmillan.

Werner, P. (1989). Teaching games—A tactical perspective. *Journal of Physical Education, Recreation and Dance, 60*(3), 97–101.

Werner, P., Thorpe, R., & Bunker, D. (1996). Teaching games for understanding: Evolution of a model. *Journal of Physical Education, Recreation, and Dance, 67*(1), 28–33.

Wiggins, G. P. (1993). *Assessing student behavior: Exploring the purpose and limits of testing*. San Francisco: Jossey-Bass Publishers.

Williams, A. M., & Grant, A. (1999). Training perceptual skill in sport. *International Journal of Sport Psychology, 30*, 194–220.

Williams, M., Davids, K., Burwitz, L., & Williams, J. (1993). Cognitive knowledge and soccer performance. *Perceptual and Motor Skills, 72*, 579–593.

Wrzos, J. (1984). *La tactique de l'attaque*. Bräkel: Broodcoorens.

Zessoules, R., & Gardner, H. (1991). Authentic assessment: Beyond the buzzword and into the classroom. In V. Perrone (Ed.), *Expanding student assessment* (pp. 47–71). Alexandria, VA: Association for Supervision and Curriculum Development.

Endnotes

CHAPTER 1

1. Uncertainty and certainty are related to the quantity and quality of available information. Uncertainty is the information that we do not possess about the state of the system (Atlan, 1979).

CHAPTER 3

1. For more details on the systemic analysis of team sports, see Gréhaigne & Godbout (1995).

CHAPTER 4

1. See French & McPherson (1999) and McPherson (1999) for more details on the recent development of the *action plan profile* and *current event profile* constructs.

CHAPTER 5

1. A class of game play problems is defined by the similarity between the practical knowledge involved the problem solving modes in which the student/athlete must rely upon in order to respond to the different problems faced in different game situations.

CHAPTER 8

1. For information on the TSAP-volleyball, refer to Richard, Godbout, & Griffin (2002).

Index

A

Accountability of students, 163
Acquisition through action, 138–139
Action rules
  acquisition through, 138–139
  defensive, *52*
  definition of, 50, 53
  emergence of, 53–54
  motor capacities and, 55
  offensive, *51*
  play organization and, 55, *56*
  principles of action based on, 56
  use, 54–55
Adaptation and learning in relation to team games and sports, 144–152
Allal, 74
Almond, 4, 77, 103
Analytical model of game play analysis, 8–9
Anzieu, 151
Apprenticeship, 104–107
Appropriation and exploration, 117
Atlan, 12
Attack *versus* defense in team sports, 6, 18–20
Avallon Project, 120–122

B

Bailey, 77, 103
Ball
  exchange complexity, 70–72
  location, 62–63
  possession indices, 80–81
Barbier, 138
Barrow, 76
Basketball, 148
Baumgartner, 76
Bengoechea, 125
Bernard, 152
Billard, 49
Blomquist, 77
Bourdieu, 53
Bouthier, 27, 38, 90
Brackenridge, 7
Brousseau, 115
Brown, 75
Bunker, 125–126

C

Cardinet, 74
Carron, 151
Caverni, 114
Chamberlain, 40
Chapuis, 151
Choice of motor skills, 6

Classification of sports
and games, 3–5
Closed and open systems, 13
Cobb, 106
Coelho, 40
Cognitive maps, players', 44, 46
Cognitivist perspective, 104
Cohesion principle, 31
Collective aspects
of decision-making, 45–47
Collective dimension, 151
Common traits in games
and sports, 141–144
Community of practice, 161–162
Competency
networks, 26–27, 45–46
principle, 31–32
Configuration of play, 35–37, 134
perceived, 59–60
Constructivism, 98, 104, 106, 108,
161–162
Covered play-spaces, 65
Critical thinking strategies, 112–116
Current assessment practices
in team sports, 75–78

D

Debates
of ideas, 116–118
strategies for encouraging,
112–116
technical/tactical, 119–122
verbalization and, 114–116
Deception principle, 30–31
Decision-making in team sports
adaptability in, 144–152
based on expertise, 40–41
challenges of, 38–40
collective aspects of, 45–47
configuration of play and, 35–37
elements involved in, 42–43
factors affecting individual,
38–39
individual aspects of, 44–45
Mahlo's model of, 124–125

practical knowledge and, 177
research on, 40–42
Tactical-Decision Learning
Model, 128–129
Teaching Game for Understand-
ing model, 125–128
translation into play, 39–40
Deductive logic, 127
Defensive action rules, *51*
Deleplace, 3, 7
model of analysis, 18–20
Deriaz, 117
Distribution, dominant, 62–63
Dominant distribution
of players, 62–64
Dynamic approach to observation
of game play, 64–65

E

Economy principle, 32
Effective play-spaces, 62–63, 70
Elements of decision-making,
42–43
Emergence of action rules, 53–54
Ericsson, 114
Ethics, sport, 152–153
European handball, 146–147
Exchanges, ball, 70–72
Expertise
information-processing and, 159
and practice, 42

F

Facets of performance assessment
in team sports, 74–75
Feschbach, 117
Fielding/scoring games, 4–5
Force ratio, 6, 23–26, 32, 151
decision-making and, 45–46
perceived configuration
of play and, 59
Formative assessment
authentic team sport, 79–80
indices, 80–86

teaching-learning process and, 78–79
using volume of play, 82–86
French, 41, 118, 159, 177
French model of team sports, 18–20
Functional dimension, 14–15

G

Game Performance Assessment Instrument, 77, 94–97
Game play
analysis models, 8–10
configuration, 35–37
decision making and practical knowledge in, 177
observational analysis of, 60–65, 107–111
structuralist analysis of, 9
systemic analysis of, 9–10
transformation during, 136–140
Godbout, 28, 74, 75–76, 77, 90, 93, 114, 177
Good, 105
Grant, 41
Graydon, 42–43
Gréhaigne, 4–5, 7, 28, 45, 49, 50, 77, 80–81, 90, 114, 151, 158, 177
Griffin, 177
Grouping of students, 163
Guillon, 49

H

Halbvachs, 50
Handball, European, 146–147
Hoc, 114
Holt, 125–126
Homogeneity of systems, 17–18
Hughes, 103

I

Importance of performance assessment in team sports, 74
Improvement principle, 32

Individual and collective strategies, 7
Individual aspects of decision-making, 44–45
Inductive logic, 127
Information
collection for formative assessment, 79
problems in team sports, 7–8, 163–164
processing research, 158–160
uncertainty about, 177
Integration and generalization, 118
Invasion games, 4–5
content of tactical knowledge in, 49–50
Game Performance Assessment Instrument for, 95–97
internal logic of playing, 23–26
systemic analysis of, 11
Team Sport Assessment Procedure for, 90–94

J

Jackson, 76
Janis, 117
Journal of Teaching in Physical Education, 125

K

Kirk, 125–126, 161–162
Knowledge bases, players', 44, 46
Knowledge of performance, 75
Knowledge of results, 75

L

Labate, 112
Lave, 161
Learning, regulation of, 79
Learning process in team sports, the. *See also* Teaching team sports
adaptation and, 144–152

interesting and challenging
  activities in, 163
Mahlo's model and tactical
  approach, 124–125
making sense out of, 129–130
prior and current models of,
  123–128
Tactical-Decision Learning
  Model, 128–129
Teaching Game for Understanding
  model, 125–128
transformation, 136–140
Leplat, 114, 138
Lewin, 151
Liberty of action, 4
Location
  ball, 62–63
  player, 44–45
Logic, 127, 143–144
Long-term practice, 42

M

Macdonald, 160, 161–162
MacPhail, 126
Magill, 41–42
Mahlo's Model, 124–125
Malglaive, 50
Manipulation, range of, 66–68
Martin, 151
Martinek, 77
McBride, 112
McGee, 76, 77
McMorris, 42–43
McPherson, 41, 118, 159, 177
Mérand, 151
Mitchell, 77, 97
Mobility principle, 31
Modeling of students' play in team
  sports in secondary school,
  130–136
Motivations for play, 130
Motor capacities
  action rules and, 55
  choice of, 6
  decision-making and, 38–40

emergence of action rules and,
  53–54
tactical knowledge learning and,
  80

N

Net/wall games, 4–5

O

Observational analysis of game play
  ball location, effective play-space,
    and dominant distribution,
    62–64
  dynamic approach to, 64–65
  static approach to, 60–62
  teaching-learning, 107–111
  training in, 86–87
Offensive action rules, 51
Open-ended questions, 113
Opportunity principle, 31
Opposition relationships
  in team sports, 7, 15–17
  force ratio of, 6, 23–26
  organization levels in, 24–26
Organization
  competency network and, 26–27
  levels, 24–26
  mode of secondary school
    students, 131–133
  problems in team sports, 8
  rules, play, 55, 56
Oslin, 97

P

Passing and shooting, 68–72
Pedagogical implications of
  assessment, 97–99
Pedagogical principles of
  Tactical-Decision Learning
  Model, 162–163
Perception
  and configuration of play, 59–60
  decision-making and, 41–42, 43

Performance assessment
    in team sports
    current practices, 75–78
    facets of, 74–75
    Game Performance Assessment
        Instrument, 77, 94–97
    importance of, 74
    numerical indices for, 78–86
    pedagogical implications of,
        97–99
    Team Sport Assessment
        Procedure, 77, 90–94
Perkins, 112, 161
Perrenoud, 74
Physical engagement, rules, 4
Picard, 93
Pinheiro, 77
Play
    childhood, 10
    configurations of, 35–37, 59–60,
        134
    modeling secondary school team
        sports, 130–136
    motivations for, 130
    space, effective, 62–63, 70, 131
    volume of, 82–86
Players
    areas occupied by, 135–136
    cognitive maps, 44, 46
    competency networks, 26–27
    development of knowledge
        and action rules, 54–55
    dominant distribution of, 62–64
    knowledge bases, 44, 46
    location and posture, 44–45
    posture, 44–45, 66–68
    resources, 44, 46
    rights, 4
    tactical decisions by, 28–29
    transformations, 136–140
Plummer, 152
Positional attack, 31
Posture, player, 44–45, 66–68
Poussin, 117
Practical knowledge and
        decision-making, 177

Practice
    community of, 161–162
    and expertise, 42
    -theory-practice model, 143–144

R

Range of manipulation, 66–68
Rapport of strength, 23–26
Rating of performances, 76
Reality and game play, 3–4
Reciprocal attacks, 32
Regulation
    of learning, 79
    principles, 15
Reproducing solutions, 143
Research and development
    on decision-making and sports,
        40–42
    on development of learners'
        game knowledge, 157–160
    implications for learning
        and instruction, 163–164
    information-processing,
        158–160, 163–164
    situated learning theory,
        160–163
Reserve principle, 32
Rethinking Teaching Games, 4
Reversibility, 144
Richard, 81, 93, 177
Rink, 157
Rioux, 151
Roche, 7, 49
Rouchier, 50
Rougeau, 152
Routines, 138–140
Rules, fundamental, 4

S

Safrit, 76
Schunk, 114
Schwager, 112
Scoring, rules, 4
Selective attention, 41–42

Settings, teaching-learning,
    104–106
Single-player indices, 82
Situated learning theory, 160–163
Situation potential, 37
Soccer
    adaptation in relation to,
        147–148
    assessment implications for, 98
    passing and shooting in, 68–72
    player distribution in, 63
    range of manipulation in, 66–68
    structural and functional
        dimensions of, 14–15
    team indices for, 80–81
Space and time problems
    in team sports, 7
Specificity, 141–142
Sports and games, classification of,
    3–5
Stability, 144, 152
Standardized testing, 76
Static approach to observation
    of game play, 60–62
Static-phase, 29
Statistics derived from
    competition, 76
Strategy
    collective, 45
    individual, 44
    players decisions using, 27–30
    principles underlying, 30–33
Strean, 125
Structural dimension, 14
Structuralist model of game play
    analysis, 9
Students
    accountability, 163
    as active learners, 162
    exploration by, 112–113
    grouping of, 163
Subsystems, semi-isolated, 13
Support organization of play, 32
Surprise principle, 31
Systemic model of game play
    analysis, 9–10

System of play, 8
Systems
    closed and open, 13
    Deleplace model of, 18–20
    general properties of, 12–13
    homogeneity of, 17–18
    regulation, 15
    subsystems and, 13
    theory of dynamic, 11–12
    time and, 14–15
    uncertainty, 177

T

Tactical knowledge
    action rules and, 50–55
    approach to team sports, 18–20
    content of, 49–50
    debates, 119–122
    decision-making and, 44, 46
    Mahlo's model and, 124–125
    motor capacities and, 55, 80
    principles of action based on, 56
    strategy and, 27–30
    Tactical-Decision Learning
        Model and, 128–129, 155–164
Target games, 4–5
Teaching Game for Understanding,
    125–128
Teaching team sports. see also
    Learning process in team
        sports, the
    adaptation and learning
        in relation to, 144–152
    Avallon Project, 120–122
    and common traits in games
        and sports, 141–144
    conception of apprenticeship in,
        104–107
    critical issues in, 141–153
    critical thinking in, 112–116
    debate-of-ideas in, 112–118
    and ethics, 152–153
    and formative assessment, 78–79
    management of classes for
        optimal learning in, 148–152

observational approach of game play and, 107–111

practice-theory-practice model and, 143–144

reproducing solutions and constructing new responses in, 143

reversibility and stability in, 144

settings, 104–106

stages between doing and understanding in, 118–119

team dynamics in, 149–150

using the Game Performance Assessment Instrument in, 95–97

using the Team Sport Assessment Procedure in, 92–94

Team dynamics, 149–150

Team indices, 80–82

Team Sport Assessment Procedure, 77, 90–94

Technical/tactical debates, 119–122

Theory and practice, 143–144

Thomas, 159

Thorpe, 125–126

Time and systems, 14–15

Tishman, 112

Transformation, 136–140

Transversality, 141–142

Tritschler, 76

Turner, 77

U

Uncertainty, 177

V

Validation, 117

Veal, 74, 75, 78

Verbalization, 42, 114–116

Vergnaud, 50

Volume of play, 82–86

Von Clausewitz, 27

W

Walliser, 12

Wenger, 161

Werner, 77

Williams, 41

Wood, 76